SERIES EDITOR: MARTIN WINDROW

MEN-AT-ARMS 344

THE TRIBES OF THE SIOUX NATION

TEXT BY
MICHAEL JOHNSON
COLOUR PLATES BY
JONATHAN SMITH

OSPREY

First published in 2000 by Osprey Publishing,
Elms Court, Chapel Way, Botley, Oxford, OX2 9LP

ISBN 1 85532 878 X

Editor: Martin Windrow
Design: Alan Hamp
Originated by Colourpath, London, UK
Printed in China through World Print Ltd

00 01 02 03 04 10 9 8 7 6 5 4 3 2 1

FOR A CATALOGUE OF ALL TITLES PUBLISHED BY OSPREY MILITARY, AUTOMOTIVE AND AVIATION PLEASE WRITE TO:

The Marketing Manager, Osprey Publishing Ltd, PO Box 140, Wellingborough, Northants NN8 4ZA, United Kingdom
Email: **info@ospreydirect.co.uk**

The Marketing Manager, Osprey Direct USA, PO Box 130, Sterling Heights, MI 48311-0310, USA
Email: **info@ospreydirectusa.com**

Or visit the Osprey website at: **www.ospreypublishing.com**

Dedication

This book is dedicated to my wife Nancy and daughters Sarah and Pauline, for their help and encouragement over the years.

Acknowledgements

The author would like to thank Timothy O'Sullivan and Denise Payne for their help in the preparation of the text. The following people have been helpful and stimulating with their comments: Rosemary and the late Dennis Lessard, who lived on the Rosebud Reservation, South Dakota; the late Dr James H Howard, Stillwater, Oklahoma; Louis Garcia of Ft Totten Reservation, North Dakota; Dr Colin Taylor, Hastings, UK; Samuel Cahoon, Warren, New Jersey; Neil Gilbert, Ipswich, UK; and Richard Green of Birmingham, UK.

Artist's Note

Readers may care to note that the original paintings from which the colour plates in this book were prepared are available for private sale. All reproduction copyright whatsoever is retained by the Publishers. All enquiries should be addressed to:

Jonathan Smith, 38 Albert Street, Cheltenham, Glos GL50 4HS, UK

The Publishers regret that they can enter into no correspondence upon this matter.

THE TRIBES OF THE SIOUX NATION

INTRODUCTION

THE SIOUX are perhaps the most famous tribe of North American Indians. Their western branch, the Teton division, were probably the most powerful and numerous of the so-called Plains Indian peoples. The Plains Indians, who were dependent upon the horse for mobility and the bison for food, were a mix of older cultural traditions reformed by recent migration to the Plains ecological area. Woodland Algonkians, followed later by other northern forest relatives, occupied the northern Plains (Blackfoot, Cheyenne, Arapaho), whilst the partly horticultural Siouan-speaking tribes already occupied the Missouri valley, adding to the Caddoan people (Pawnee), who were long-time horticultural occupants of the area.

It would seem that by 1700 AD some Sioux had moved west from their traditional homes on the Mississippi River to the Lake Traverse region of present-day South Dakota; by 1780 they were ranging on the west side of the Missouri River and had penetrated as far west as the Black Hills. Other peoples moved to the High Plains from the west (Comanche) and north (Plains Apache), and there were some whose ancestors had probably eked out an existence on the margins of the area. The mobility now granted by the acquisition of the horse had transformed Indian life. Horses were introduced to the south-western tribes in the 17th century by the Spanish colonists, and had spread north via intertribal trade, ultimately forming vast herds of hardy wild ponies. Tribal groups travelled widely following the herds of bison which now provided basic food, supplemented by deer, pronghorn antelope and wild foods. A few still raised vegetables from small gardens. Some tribes remained horticulturists (Mandan, Hidatsa), others quickly adopted a completely nomadic High Plains culture (Crow).

The Sioux have a tradition that at one time the whole people resided within the present state of Minnesota, originally at Mille Lacs and later near the confluence of the Mississippi and Minnesota rivers for several generations. They were first reported by the French explorer Jean Nicolet in 1640, although the first actual meeting between Europeans and the Sioux probably occurred some 20 years later when the explorers Radisson and Groseilliers spent a winter of near-starvation – probably in eastern Minnesota – when visited by some Sioux. As a result of pressure from the Ojibwa (Chippewa), who were armed by the French

Flying Pipe (Canupa Kinyan), Yankton Sioux, wearing a shirt with porcupine quilled strips and hair fringes. He holds an iron pipe-tomahawk and an eagle wing fan. (Photograph William Henry Jackson, c1872)

fur traders, the Sioux began a movement westward. Coincidentally horses were obtained in trade and war by their western bands, which hastened the transfer from a mixed horticultural and hunting Prairie economy to a truly nomadic High Plains culture. Whilst the change was ultimately complete for the numerous western branch of the Sioux – the Teton Sioux – other branches remained largely marginal.

There were seven branches of the people called Sioux, a name derived from a French corruption of the Ojibwa (Chippewa) term *nadowe-is-iw-ug* meaning 'small adder' or 'enemy'- a derogatory term applied by their traditional enemies. Sometimes the tribe as a whole are termed *Dakota* or the slight variations of that word in the three varying dialects of the language spoken by the tribe – *Dakota*, *Nakota* and *Lakota*. In the English language (and despite its origin) the name 'Sioux' is the more correct term to describe the whole or any component part of the people, except when referring to their linguistic divisions. (However, see note on nomenclature opposite).

The term *Dakota* is said to mean 'allies', and correctly refers to the language spoken by the seven sub-tribes, a member of the so-called Siouan linguistic family widely spoken by several tribes in the Mississippi and Missouri river valleys (and a divergent branch in the Carolinas). The Dakota language is divided into three dialects. The eastern or *Dakota* proper was spoken by the four sub-tribes who remained within the present boundaries of Minnesota – the Mdewakanton, Wahpekute, Sisseton and Wahpeton. The *Nakota* dialect was spoken by the middle division – two sub-tribes, the Yankton and Yanktonai. The western or *Lakota* dialect was spoken by a single sub-tribe, the Teton. The terms Dakota, Nakota and Lakota were once employed by the speakers of the three dialects to identify both their own dialect and the language of the entire Sioux tribe.

The original seven sub-tribes, when living in their traditional eastern location, were also sometimes called the 'Seven Council Fires'. All seven were further divided into bands. The Teton branch – the largest division of the Sioux, outnumbering the other six together – was divided into seven large bands each sometimes large enough to be considered a sub-tribe itself. As far as can be determined, the Sioux as a whole probably always numbered between 35,000 and 50,000 people of which two-thirds were Teton or Western Sioux. Today perhaps 80,000 descendants are enrolled at various reservations, about half resident. However, the numbers of full-bloods are rapidly decreasing, and probably stand at less than 25% of that total today.

Note on nomenclature

The term *Sioux* first recorded by Nicolet in 1640 became a substitute for *Oceti Sakowin*, 'seven fireplaces' i.e. Seven Council Fires. Sioux, like Cree and Ojibwa, became the English names for whole tribes through common usage, despite the huge area of geographical distribution and numerous branches and dialectic variations which came to be recognised for each. Lakota, Nakota and Dakota are native terms in the three dialects for the Sioux as a whole; despite their constant misuse, they are not separate tribal names. The careless use of the suffix '-Sioux' to describe constituent parts of the tribe, e.g. Teton Sioux or Oglala Sioux is incorrect; these would suggest a parallel status within the tribe, when the Oglala are a sub-group of the Teton.

Despite its use in the title of this book, I have also generally avoided in the text the term 'nation', which strictly speaking suggests a united society and a political state involving coercion rather than cohesion. I am, however, fully conscious of the fact that in recent times reservation tribal communities under various influences, internal and external, have used the term in order to meet the perceived requirements of the 'Predominant Society'.

The geographical terms 'Eastern Sioux' and 'Western Sioux' would seem adequate, while such terms as Dakota Sioux, Lakota Sioux, Teton Lakota, Oglala Lakota Nation etc. are strictly wrong and confusing designations. The most cogent examination of this problem is that by Powers (1975 – see Bibliography); he suggests that Teton and Oglala are perfectly adequate designations in themselves; the Indians after all knew who they were, and we should at least attempt an understanding of their tribal structure.

In very recent times Western Sioux, particularly those living in South Dakota, have adopted 'Lakota' – their dialectic name – as a tribal name, since they view 'Sioux' as a Euro-American and derogatory term. Nevertheless, for the sake of consistency I have retained in this text 'Sioux' as the historic English language name for the tribe.

Big Head, Upper Yanktonai Sioux, c1872. He holds a pipe and an eagle feather fan, and wears a fur turban, fur-wrapped braids and beaded blanket strip. (Photograph, author's collection)

Sioux tribal structure

The seven branches of the Sioux people are as follows, divided into their three dialectic divisions A, B & C.
NB: For details of present-day reservation populations, see Table B on page 9.

(A) Eastern Sioux or Dakota dialectic division
(Also known as *Santee*, from *Isanyati* – 'dwellers at a knife shaped lake', an ancient village at Mille Lacs – although some historians believe this term should only apply to the first two sub-tribes.)
(1) Mdewakanton
'Spirit Lake Dwellers', said to have taken their name from their former homes at Mille Lacs in present eastern Minnesota, and along the Rum River, as far south as Red Wing on the Mississippi River. The Mdewakanton, with the Wahpekute, were sometimes referred to as the 'Lower Council'. They had several village bands, the Kiyuksa and Kapozha the most prominent. By treaties with the USA in 1837 and 1851 they ceded all their lands east of the Mississippi for a reservation along the Minnesota River. However, following shabby treatment by both settlers and government they were the principal participants in the Minnesota uprising of 1862-63, after which they moved west of the Missouri River or fled to Canada, although a few re-established themselves in

Minnesota. Their descendants have largely merged with other Santees but they probably predominate on the old Santee-Niobrara Reservation, Nebraska, and in four small settlements in Minnesota. A few may have been incorporated with other Santees at Sioux Valley and Birdtail in Manitoba, Canada. They probably numbered 2,000 in around 1780; today they have about 5,000 descendants mixed with Wahpekute, mostly mixed-blood.
(2) Wahpekute
'Leaf Shooters', a branch of the Eastern Sioux who once lived on the Cannon and Blue Earth Rivers in southern Minnesota, particularly around Faribault's Trading Post. In early 1857 a few Wahpekutes under Chief Inkpaduta killed a number of white settlers in the Spirit Lake region of north-western Iowa. The Wahpekutes had been split by dissension since about 1840, and some had not taken part in the treaties of 1851 when required to move to the Lower Agency of their reservation along the Minnesota River. They were sometimes known as the 'Lower Council Sioux', together with the Mdewakanton. After the uprising of 1862-63 the Wahpekutes mainly joined the various Mdewakanton bands, mostly at Crow Creek Reservation, South Dakota, and moved later to Niobrara, Nebraska, but never again reported as a separate tribe. Their

(continued on page 7)

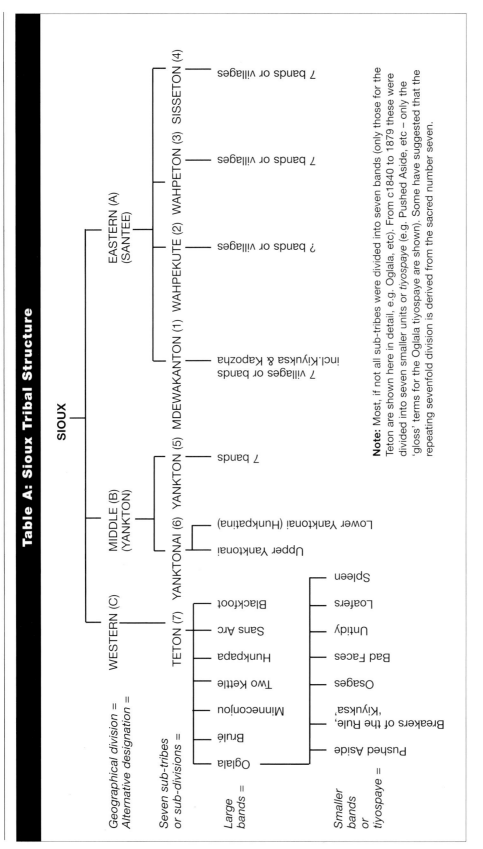

Table A: Sioux Tribal Structure

SIOUX

EASTERN (A) (SANTEE)

- MDEWAKANTON (1) — 7 villages or bands incl.Kiyuksa & Kapozha
- WAHPEKUTE (1) — ? bands or villages
- WAHPETON (2) — 7 bands or villages
- WAHPETON (3) — 7 bands or villages
- SISSETON (4) — 7 bands or villages

MIDDLE (B) (YANKTON)

- YANKTON (5) — 7 bands
- YANKTONAI (6)
  - Upper Yanktonai
  - Lower Yanktonai (Hunkpatina)

WESTERN (C)

- TETON (7)

Geographical division =
Alternative designation =

Seven sub-tribes
or sub-divisions =

Large bands =
- Oglala
- Brulé
- Minneconjou
- Two Kettle
- Hunkpapa
- Sans Arc
- Blackfoot

Smaller bands or tiyospaye =
- Pushed Aside
- Breakers of the Rule, 'Kiyuksa'
- Osages
- Bad Faces
- Untidy
- Loafers
- Spleen

Note: Most, if not all sub-tribes were divided into seven bands (only those for the Teton are shown here in detail, e.g. Oglala, etc). From c1840 to 1879 these were divided into seven smaller units or tiyospaye (e.g. Pushed Aside, etc – only the 'gloss' terms for the Oglala tiyospaye are shown). Some have suggested that the repeating sevenfold division is derived from the sacred number seven.

Saskatchewan. They originally numbered about 1,500; today there are perhaps 15,000 Wahpeton-Sisseton descendants, including about 8,000, mainly mixed-blood, at Lake Traverse and Devil's Lake.

(4) Sisseton

'Ridges of Fish Offal Dwellers'. The principal location of the Sisseton before 1851 was near Traverse des Sioux and at the junctions of the Cottonwood and Blue Earth rivers with the Minnesota River around present-day New Ulm and Mankato, Minnesota. However, by the 1840s some had already moved to the Lake Traverse and James River country. Others settled with the Wahpeton about Upper Agency on the Minnesota River after the treaty of 1851, known as 'Upper Council Sioux'. The reservation was reduced in area in 1858, beginning the events which led to the uprising of August 1862 under the Mdewakanton Chief Little Crow, and the defeat and dispersal of the Santee which followed. The Sissetons' descendants are largely combined with the Wahpetons at Lake Traverse, South Dakota, with smaller groups at Devil's Lake, North Dakota, and in Canada at Moose Woods and Standing Buffalo, Saskatchewan, with a few intermixed on the other reserves. They numbered about 2,500 in 1830.

(continued from page 5)

descendants have combined with their relatives on the Santee-Niobrara Reservation, Nebraska, at Sioux Valley and Oak Lake, Manitoba, and a few at Round Plain, Saskatchewan, Fort Peck, Montana, and in all communities with Mdewakantons. They were estimated at 800 in 1824; today they have merged with the Mdewakanton, the largest group being 750 at Santee, Nebraska, but mostly mixed-blood. A colony of this group established themselves at Flandreau, South Dakota.

(3) Wahpeton

'Dwellers among the Leaves'. The traditional home of the Wahpetons was on the Minnesota River above Traverse des Sioux, but after 1851 they removed to the Lac-qui-Parle and Big Stone Lake districts above the Upper Agency of the reservation established on the Minnesota River for all Santee Sioux. They were, together with the Sissetons, sometimes called 'Upper Council Sioux'. They took part in the uprising of 1862-63, as a result of which they were widely scattered. The largest group ultimately joined the Sisseton on the Lake Traverse Reservation, South Dakota, with smaller groups at Devil's Lake, North Dakota; Birdtail, Long Plain and Oak Lake, Manitoba; and Standing Buffalo and Round Plain,

(B) Middle Sioux or Nakota dialectic division

(5) Yankton

'End Village'. In 1804 the Lewis and Clark expedition found the Yankton Sioux in the vicinity of the Big Sioux and James rivers above their junction with the Missouri; but they and their close relatives the Yanktonai were first noted by early French traders in the Mille Lacs area and later in the vicinity of modern Sioux City, Iowa. In 1858 they ceded all their lands excepting a reservation on the north bank of the Missouri near the present town of Wagner, South Dakota. They were divided into seven bands, and later an eighth, the 'half-breed band', was added. The Yanktons have long been residents of their South Dakota reservation, but the so-called 'Yankton' at Fort Peck, Montana, are for the most part actually Yanktonai. The Yankton probably numbered 4,500 in c1804, a figure halved during the 19th century; today about 3,400 descendants live on their old reservation near Wagner.

(6) Yanktonai

'Little End Village'. The northern branch of the middle or Nakota division of the Sioux, living on both sides of the James River in the eastern parts of present South and North Dakota. They were further divided into the Upper Yanktonai, who included a sub-group Pabaska 'Cut Heads', and the Lower Yanktonai or Hunkpatina 'Campers at the Horn'. Culturally they were similar to the 'Upper Sioux' of the Santee, the Sisseton and Wahpeton, and heavily intermarried with them. A band of Kiyuksas, probably of Mdewakanton origin, were also associated with them at one time. They were probably in the Mille Lacs vicinity during the 17th century when a division within the tribe saw a portion move to Canada, becoming known as Assiniboine, Nakoda, or 'Stone Sioux' (Stoney), who thenceforth have been regarded as a separate people. The Yanktonai chief Wanata (Wanatan) joined his father Chief Red Thunder and the British trader Robert Dickson to fight the Americans in 1812; he became the most important chieftain during their early association with the Missouri traders. After 1820 he supported the American traders and extended his influence to some of the Teton bands of Saones (northern Tetons). The presence of the traders on the middle Missouri saw the growing dependence of the Teton Sioux and the redundancy of the old Sioux trade fair system originally in Yanktonai territory. In 1865 both Yanktonai branches made treaties of peace with the US and gathered on reservations. The Upper Yanktonai gradually located on the northern half of the Standing Rock Reservation and at Devil's Lake in North Dakota, these being mostly Pabaska; the Lower Yanktonai moved to the Crow Creek Reservation in South Dakota and Fort Peck, Montana. All groups are heavily intermarried with Sisseton and Wahpeton, and a few accompanied them to Canada. Today they have about 12,000 descendants.

(C) Western Sioux or Lakota dialectic division

(7) Teton

'Dwellers-on-the-Plains', the largest sub-division of the Sioux, who no doubt resided at one time within the boundaries of Minnesota, but who had crossed the Missouri by 1750 to become the most numerous and formidable of the nomadic equestrian High Plains peoples. When the US government sent Lewis and Clark to explore parts of the lands newly acquired by the Louisiana Purchase in 1804, they found them in four separate sub-tribes on both sides of the Missouri River: the Brulé between the White and Bad rivers, the Oglala (at this period also known by their Santee name, Okandada) between the Bad and Cheyenne rivers, the Minneconjou below the Moreau River, and the Saone on the Grand River northwards. There can be little doubt that the subsequent increase in population was in part due to the adoption of eastern groups. For instance, the Oglala incorporated several immigrant groups after 1805 including the Kiyuksas, originally a band of Mdewakanton who had first joined, then left, the Yanktonai, and the Wazhazhe band of Brulé who intermarried with Ponca and Osage.

At the time Lewis and Clark were on the upper Missouri, of the Saones (northern Tetons) only the Minneconjou had assumed the status of a separate people; and by the time of the Atkinson-O'Fallon Treaty of 1825, which asserted friendship between the United States and the Missouri River tribes, the commissioners lumped the Minneconjous with the sub-tribes now known as Sans Arcs and Two Kettles. It is evident that at this time a main Teton trading post before the establishment of Laramie was Fort Tecumseh (later Fort Pierre), and the place where they met the Atkinson-O'Fallon Commission was at the mouth of the Bad River. The commission's report states that the Saones were divided into two groups: one the Minneconjous, Sans Arcs and Two Kettles west of the Missouri, the other the 'Fire Hearts Band' (Blackfoot Sioux) on the east bank. The seven large bands of the Teton, recognised as independent before the establishment of The Great Sioux Reservation in 1868, were:

a. Oglala, 'They-Scatter-Their-Own'
b. Brulé or Sicangu, 'Burnt-Thighs'
c. Minneconjou, 'Planters-Beside-the-Water'
d. Two Kettle or Oohenonpa
e. Hunkpapa, 'Campers-at-the-Horn' (or end of the camp circle)
f. Sans Arc or Itazipco, 'Those-Without-Bows'
g. Blackfoot or Sihasapa (not to be confused with the Blackfoot tribe of Montana and Alberta).

After the break-up of The Great Sioux Reservation into smaller reservations following the surrender of many groups after the Indian Wars, the Oglala were assigned to the Pine Ridge Reservation, South Dakota, with a few in the Milk's Camp Community on the Rosebud Reservation. The Brulé went to the Rosebud (Upper Brulé) and Lower Brulé reservations, South Dakota; the Minneconjou, Sans Arc and Two Kettle to Cheyenne River, South Dakota; the Blackfoot to Cheyenne River and Standing Rock, North and South Dakota; and the Hunkpapa to Standing Rock, Fort Peck, Montana, and Wood Mountain, Saskatchewan.

During the early 19th century the Teton population probably exceeded 30,000, which reduced somewhat during the early reservation period. Today there are perhaps 50,000 or more descendants, of which about half live on reservations – about 35% full-blood, Pine Ridge and Rosebud reservations having the largest numbers. A large number are also to be found in several cities.

Rain-in-the-Face, Hunkpapa Sioux, c.1902. He was born in c1835, and so named after a fight with a Cheyenne who spattered his face with blood. Many times on the warpath, he was one of the party which killed Capt Fetterman and his command near Fort Phil Kearney in December 1866, and fought at Fort Totten in 1868. He joined Sittting Bull in 1874; wounded at the Little Bighorn, he fled to Canada until 1880, surrendering at Fort Keogh, Montana, and finally settling at the Standing Rock Agency. He died in September 1905. He is seen here holding a shield with bison, thunderbird and bear symbolism. Photograph by F.B.Fiske.

Table B: 20th Century Sioux Populations

Country & Province or State	Reserve or Reservation	Division	Approx. resident population 1990
Canada:			
Manitoba	Sioux Village	Wahpeton	300
	Long Plain (Portage La Prairie)	Wahpeton, Sisseton	800
	Sioux Valley (Oak River)	Sisseton, Mdewakanton, Wahpekute, Wahpeton	1,000
	Birdtail (Birtle)	Mdewakanton, Wahpeton, Yanktonai	300
	Oak Lake	Wahpekute, Wahpeton, Yanktonai	350
Saskatchewan	Standing Buffalo (Fort Qu'Appelle)	Sisseton, Wahpeton	600
	Moose Woods (Dundurn)	Sisseton	200
	Sioux Wahpeton (Round Plain)	Wahpeton	100
	Wood Mountain	Hunkpapa	100
USA:			
Montana	Fort Peck*	Lower Yanktonai, Wahpekute, Sisseton, Wahpeton	2,000
North Dakota	Devil's Lake (Fort Totten)	Wahpeton, Sisseton, Upper Yanktonai	3,000
South Dakota	Standing Rock	Upper Yanktonai, Hunkpapa, Blackfoot	4,000
	Lake Traverse	Sisseton, Wahpeton	5,000
	Flandreau	Wahpeton	300
	Cheyenne River	Minneconjou, Blackfoot, Two Kettle, Sans Arc	3,000
	Crow Creek	Lower Yanktonai	2,000
	Lower Brulé	Brulé	1,000
	Yankton	Yankton	2,000
	Pine Ridge	Oglala, few Brulé	12,000
	Rosebud	Brulé, few Oglala	9,000
Minnesota	Upper Sioux	Mdewakanton, Sisseton, Wahpeton	200
	Lower Sioux	Mdewakanton, Wahpekute	300
	Prior Lake	Mdewakanton, Wahpekute	200
	Prairie Island	Mdewakanton, Wahpekute	200
Nebraska	Santee	Mdewakanton, Wahpekute	1,000
Total Sioux population on, or adjacent to, reserves			48,950

Notes
*Fort Peck Reservation is shared with the Assiniboine.
These figures exclude a large number of Sioux descendants now resident in cities such as Denver

THE RISE OF THE TETON SIOUX

The earliest Sioux village known to Europeans was Isanti, evidently a large settlement on the shore of Lake Mille Lacs in modern Minnesota, probably wholly or largely populated by Mdewakanton Sioux. By about 1700 or a little later migration of various groups from the region had left Isanti exposed to attacks from French traders and the incursions of the Ojibwa (Chippewa). From about 1735 Mdewakantons retreated down to the Mississippi and established a new settlement called Tintatonwan, perhaps in recognition of the former inhabitants – the Teton, who were already moving westwards. After the French and Indian War of 1754-63 the Sioux were exposed to contacts with the British victors. In 1766 they were visited by British explorer Jonathan Carver, and in 1773-75 by Peter Pond, who have left us descriptions of Sioux customs of that time. The most important leader we hear about after 1770 from Tintatonwan was Wapasha or 'Red Head-dress', who helped the British during the American Revolution. After 1783 the settlement gradually lost its importance, becoming dependent upon its more powerful neighbours; many moved west to join the Yanktonai in the upper Minnesota Valley and reinforced the emerging Western Sioux beyond.

By 1800 considerable changes had taken place in Sioux culture, particularly amongst the Eastern division. These are evident from a dependence on the trade system with British and American fur companies, and the adoption of tools, weapons and utensils; even the use of skin clothes had partially given way to traded cloth and blankets. Some Eastern Sioux still had permanent villages of bark houses, and used skin *tipis* when moving in search of game. Food still consisted of deer, elk and bison in the west; wild rice was collected in the east, and some corn was still planted.

With the transfer of the West to the United States following the Louisiana Purchase of 1803, the Santees' first official relations with the US began with Zebulon Pike's expedition of 1805-06, which established sovereignty over the area where British traders had continued to operate since the Revolution. In the West, Lewis and Clark obtained information from traders and Indians along the Missouri River, where a large portion of Sioux were now centred – the Brulé and Oglala west of the river, the Saone on both sides. The diaspora from Tintatonwan and other eastern Sioux villages was increasing the population of the emerging Teton, whose camp circles incorporated these immigrants. Links between the Yanktonai and Teton were maintained through trading; a great annual trade fair was held on the James River, bringing goods down from British Canada. Individuals and small bands could pass freely from sub-tribe to sub-tribe – e.g. Mdewakantons

Lost Medicine *(Wakantaninsni)*, Hunkpapa Sioux, 1872, holding a sabre and tobacco bag. He wears a short 'hairpipe' breastplate – this is one of the earliest known photographs of Sioux wearing 'hairpipes'. Photographed in Washington, DC, by Alexander Gardner.

Some Sioux leaders

Many of the leading figures of the mid- to late 19th century will be found among the accompanying photographs. Others include the following:

Crazy Horse, Oglala Born in 1841 or 1842, of a holy man of the same name and a sister of the Brulé warrior Spotted Tail – see caption, page 19. He was present at a number of fights at an early age, and many more in his maturity; he led the decoys in the Fetterman battle and was at the Wagon Box Fight. He proved himself a bold and adventurous war leader on the Yellowstone and in the Black Hills during the early 1870s. Surprised by Crook in the winter of 1875, he confronted him again on the Rosebud River, Montana, on 17 June 1876, and decisively halted his advance. He subsequently joined Sitting Bull and Gall on the Little Bighorn, and after fighting against Reno's battalion helped to annihilate Custer's column. His camp was destroyed by Col Mackenzie's 4th Cavalry near the Tongue River, and he finally brought in 900 followers to the Red Cloud Agency in May 1877. On 5 September he was placed under arrest by fellow Oglalas, and was stabbed and killed while allegedly trying to escape.

John Grass or Charging Bear, Blackfoot Important leader of the Sioux on the Standing Rock Reservation. He supported the agent Maj McLaughlin in his attempts to limit the influence of Sitting Bull during the 1880s. Government agents built large frame houses for the reservation chiefs to live in, including such a home for John Grass.

Inkpaduta (Red-on-Top), Wahpekute Chief of a band of Wahpekute openly hostile to whites from the early 1850s, he had made the prairies of eastern South Dakota his home. He led an attack on settlers at Spirit Lake on the Iowa-Minnesota border in 1857. He later joined the Western Sioux, and his band was present at the battle of the Little Bighorn in June 1876.

Red Thunder, Yanktonai Chief of the Yanktonai Pabaska band, he met Lt Zebulon Pike at a great council at Prairie du Chien, Wisconsin, in 1806; Pike said he was the most finely dressed of the attending chiefs. Fought with his son Wanata – see below – alongside the British in the War of 1812 under Col Robert Dickson, who married Red Thunder's sister. He was killed fighting the Chippewa in 1823.

Joseph Renville, mixed-blood Mdewakanton Born 1779 in Kapozha; died at Lac qui Parle, 1846. After fighting on the side of the British in the War of 1812,
he later became attached to American interests. He employed former Hudson's Bay traders in the commercial Columbia Fur Company around Lake Traverse. Engaged by Dr S.R.Riggs in the translation of the Bible into Dakota, the Eastern Sioux language. Succeeded by his nephew Gabriel Renville, who was chief of the Sisseton and Wahpeton at Lake Traverse Reservation, South Dakota, after its establishment.

Standing Buffalo, Sisseton-Wahpeton Moved to Canada after the Minnesota uprising in 1862, and settled around the Portage La Prairie and Fort Garry districts. He later moved with his band to a reserve in the Qu'Appelle valley, Saskatchewan, which still bears his name. His son White Cap obtained a separate reserve near Saskatoon.

Wabasha, Mdewakanton A succession of chiefs from the Kiyuksa villages in Minnesota bore this name. The 'Great Wabasha' served the British during the American Revolution, visited Mackinaw, and was welcomed by the commandant Col De Peyser. Wabasha II came to notice when he met Lt Zebulon Pike in 1806, but nominally supported British interests during the War of 1812; he died c1855. Wabasha III signed the Laramie Treaty of 1868.

Wanata (Wanatan), Yanktonai Important Pabaska chief, son of Red Thunder, born about 1795 and served with his father on the British side – with the rank of captain – during the War of 1812. His name *Wanata*, 'The Charger', was given after he charged the Americans at the battle of Fort Sandusky, where he was wounded. After 1820 he supported American interests, and was involved in development of trade on the Missouri after leaving the Lake Traverse and James River areas. His influence later waned, however, and he was murdered by disaffected tribesmen c1848. Several other Wanatas appear subsequently, probably descendants, at Devil's Lake, North Dakota.

Young-Man-Afraid-of-His-Horses, Oglala A lieutenant of Red Cloud during the war in the Powder River buffalo country in 1866, when the US military built forts for the protection of white prospectors following the Bozeman Trail. After 1868 he settled at the agencies, and died at Pine Ridge, where he has descendants to this day.

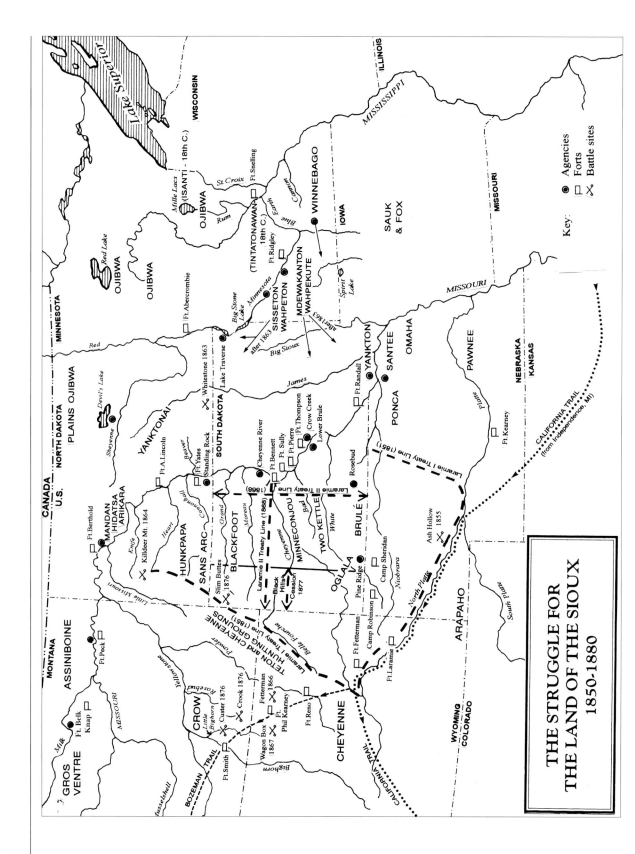

THE STRUGGLE FOR
THE LAND OF THE SIOUX
1850-1880

Key:
● Agencies
□ Forts
⚔ Battle sites

Red Cloud, Oglala Sioux, 1897. Born near the forks of the Platte River, Nebraska, in 1822, he died on the Pine Ridge Agency in December 1909. The principal war chief in the Powder River country, he led the attacks on the chain of forts (C.F.Smith, Phil Kearney and Reno) built to protect the Montana gold prospectors' route along the Bozeman Trail in the 1860s. His warriors destroyed Capt Fetterman's detachment in 1866, but he later lost many men in the Wagon Box Fight. He finally agreed to sign the 1868 Laramie Treaty after the garrisons had been abandoned, and subsequently lived at peace on the Pine Ridge Agency, taking no part in the Sioux war of 1876 and making several visits to Washington. He is seen here wearing a 'hairpipe' breastplate and eagle feather war bonnet. Photograph by D.F.Barry.

amongst the Yanktonais and Oglalas, and the Blackfoot Sioux, who were probably originally Yanktons.

How far these early official American contacts succeeded in gaining the allegiance of the Sioux is unknown; many Santees fought on the side of the British in the War of 1812. The British trader Robert Dickson attracted several chiefs to the British cause, including the renowned Wanata ('Charger'), who after the close of the war supported American interests, however. The Tetons continued to restrict the American enterprises until 1823, when Yanktons and Tetons aided the Leavenworth Expedition against the Arikaras, with whom the Sioux were always willing to fight.

At this time the Americans began to establish fur trade posts on the middle Missouri and the focal point of the trade system moved from the James River to the Missouri River; with it went the Yanktonais under Wanata, but, importantly, direct American trade also began with the Teton Sioux. With direct contact came the first treaty, by which the Indians were to recognise that they lived within the territorial limits of the United States, acknowledge their supremacy and claim their protection – the Atkinson-O'Fallon Treaty of 1825. The period 1804-25 was a time of expansion and consolidation of the Oglala and other western Sioux bands as they incorporated camps of immigrant Sioux. However, the Treaty of 1825 apparently opened up divisions between friendly and anti-American groups, until by 1850 the Oglala had divided into two factions, only to be reunited after 1870 through the establishment of the Red Cloud Agency.

After 1825 the revival of the Indian trade and competition between rival fur companies for buffalo robes began to make serious demands on the region's herds, and the migration of the Hunkpapa and Blackfoot Sioux west of the Missouri after 1830 resulted in the numbers of buffalo becoming increasingly erratic. As the Tetons moved south in the 1830s to the North Platte country, the Sioux challenged the Pawnee, killing, burning lodges, destroying crops and stealing horses. During the early 1840s there were clashes with the Shoshoni and Crow in the Bighorn Mountains region, and also with white and Indian mountain men; and by 1845 wagons with west-bound immigrants were passing up the North Platte, thinning the buffalo herds. By 1846 the US government had appointed former mountain man Thomas Fitzpatrick as Indian agent, and he helped to stop white traders bringing whisky into the Indian camps; but the summer of 1849 saw thousands of white immigrants moving along the Platte Road en route for Oregon and the California gold fields. With the white wagons came cholera, which the Indians recognised came from the white man and which they believed was spread deliberately. Teton independence was coming to an end as the US Army purchased Fort John from the American Fur Company in 1849 and installed a permanent garrison, renaming the post Fort Laramie.

From Laramie to Laramie, 1851-68

The 50 years following the Louisiana Purchase of 1803 had brought some changes to the life and culture of the Western Sioux, through contacts with explorers, traders, trappers and artists and the development of the Missouri River fur trade. However, their independent, nomadic, equestrian lifestyle remained largely intact, as it did among their closest allies the Cheyenne and Arapaho.

The events of 1849 saw a huge increase in the numbers of white settlers travelling the California Trail. This started at Independence, Missouri, swinging north-west across Kansas and Nebraska to the Platte River, then west along the North Platte to Fort Laramie, then west again over the Continental Divide. Despite the thousands who travelled the route by wagon no serious Indian attacks took place, although the slaughter of game and occasional shootings on either side of the trail caused much tension.

In 1851 the government authorised Superintendent Mitchell and the agent Fitzpatrick as commissioners in treaty negotiations which took place at Fort Laramie in late summer with the Sioux and other tribes whose lands were being traversed by hordes of gold-seekers. The treaty subsequently defined tribal boundaries; in return the Indians were to abstain from all depredations against whites passing through their country. The government promised presents and annuities. The council lasted 18 days, and was attended by thousands of Indians; harmony reigned, even between groups who were hereditary enemies.

Friction continued, however, and in 1855 following the 'Grattan massacre' – see caption, page 19 – Gen Harney was assigned to command a campaign to enforce order along the California Trail from Fort Leavenworth via old Fort Kearney on the Platte. He reached the

Sioux and Cheyenne chiefs at Fort Laramie for the council which concluded the treaty of 1868. They met the peace commissioners to negotiate the closing of the Bozeman Trail, the abandonment of Forts Reno, Phil Kearney and C.F.Smith, and the creation of The Great Sioux Reservation.
***(Left to right)* Spotted Tail, Roman Nose, Old-Man-Afraid-of-his-Horses, Lone Horn, Whistling Elk, Pipe, and Slow Bull. Photograph by Alexander Gardner.**

Blue River at Ash Hollow, Nebraska, where he attacked a camp of Brulé under Little Thunder whilst engaging the chief in a parley, killing over 130 Indians and destroying the village. Harney proceeded to Laramie and thence to Fort Pierre on the Missouri.

In 1861 gold was discovered in Montana and the flow of gold-seekers, instead of continuing west, turned north from Laramie, crossing the Powder River – the heart of Sioux buffalo country. Government obligations were left unfulfilled during the American Civil War, and none of the treaties hastily cobbled together at its close were ratified. The US Army took over protection of the Powder River Road (Bozeman Trail), building Forts Reno, Phil Kearney and C.F.Smith to keep the trail open for the gold-seekers.

Fort Phil Kearney was built in 1866 under command of Col H.B. Carrington with 2,000 men, but was constantly harassed by Oglalas and Minneconjous. In December 1866 the Indians successfully ambushed a relief force for a wood train and escort from Fort Phil Kearney under the impetuous Capt Fetterman, and in less than two hours all 90 men (from the 18th Infantry and 2nd Cavalry) were killed. When the bodies were found they had been stripped, scalped and mutilated.

The following summer, at the so-called Wagon Box Fight, another wood train from Fort Phil Kearney under Maj J.W.Powell corralled in a strong position, with wagon bodies reinforced with logs and grain sacks and manned by 40 men armed with modified Springfield breech-loading rifles. Despite several charges many hundreds of warriors failed to overrun the defensive position, and scores were swept away by the new long range firearms.

While fighting along the trail continued the Treaty Commission and the Sioux met again at Laramie, producing the Second Laramie Treaty of 1868. Red Cloud, the Oglala war leader in the Powder River country, refused to sign the treaty until the three forts were abandoned – whereupon he moved in and burned them before going on to Laramie and signing as he had promised. The abandonment of the Bozeman Trail forts constituted a kind of victory for Red Cloud. The 1868 treaty defined The Great Sioux Reservation between the 104th meridian on the west, the Missouri River on the east (plus some Santee lands on the east side of the Missouri), the 46th parallel on the north and the 43rd parallel on the south. Amongst those who signed were representatives of the Oglala, Brulé, Minneconjou, Blackfoot Sioux, Two Kettle, Sans Arcs, Hunkpapa, Yanktonai and Santee.

By 1870 around half the entire Sioux people were on reservations and drawing provisions from agencies. The Yanktons lived peaceably on their reservation in Charles Mix County, South Dakota; the Yanktonais were at Devil's Lake and Fort Yates (Upper Yanktonai) and Fort Thompson (Lower Yanktonai); the Sissetons and Wahpetons, under the Renvilles and Red Iron, were at Lake Traverse and Devil's Lake; the Minneconjous, Sans Arcs, and Two Kettles at Cheyenne River Agency (Fort Bennett); the Hunkpapas and Blackfoot Sioux at Grand River (Fort Yates); the Oglalas and Brulés under the Whetstone Agency (Fort Randall); and the Lower Brulés at Fort Thompson. A mixed group of Santees were now at Niobrara, Nebraska, and a colony of the latter group at Flandreau. In 1869-70 peace returned to Western Sioux country, and Chiefs Red Cloud and Spotted Tail made their first visits to Washington.

Four Bears, chief of the Two Kettle Sioux (top), and White Swan, chief of the Minneconjou Sioux – part of a delegation of Minneconjous, Sans Arcs and Two Kettles from Fort Bennett to Washington, DC, in May-June 1870, which also included Red Feather and Running Bull. Photographed by Gurnsey & Illingworth. (Author's collection)

THE SANTEE UPRISING, 1862-63

The so-called Sioux Uprising of 1862 left more than 500 white settlers dead; in the longer term, the hostilities launched a series of final Indian wars on the Northern Plains which culminated in the Wounded Knee tragedy of 1890.

The Eastern Sioux had a long association with whites; they had fought in the War of 1812 on the side of the British, had long been dependent upon the fur trade, and had undergone considerable cultural changes. Some professed Christianity; chiefs lived in houses and dressed as whites. The pressure from the Chippewa and the availability of horses had drawn the Santee from the lakes and forests onto the prairies of the Minnesota River valley. The treaty of 1851, signed by the Wahpetons and Sissetons at Traverse des Sioux and by the Mdewakantons and Wahpekutes at Mendota, signed away their lands in southern Minnesota in exchange for a reservation 20 miles wide and 140 miles long on both sides of the Minnesota River, divided into the Upper (Yellow Medecine) and Lower (Redwood) Agencies serving about 7,000 Indians – although not all of them moved onto the reservation. In exchange the US government was to provide various provisions, cash and annuities over a 50-year period. The Indians became ever more dependent upon the provisions of the treaty, which the government singularly failed to honour. Government payments were often late, leaving Indians in debt to traders and mixed-

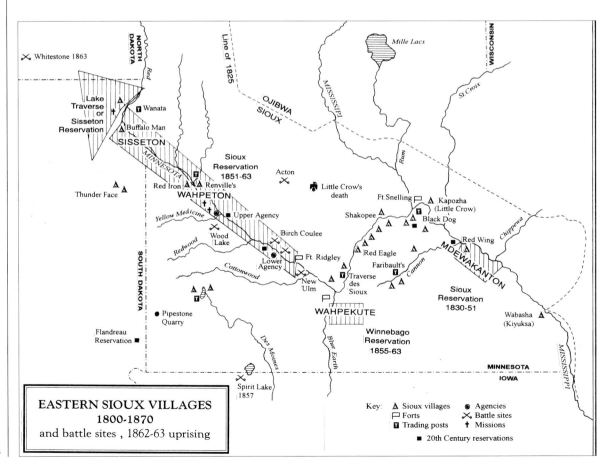

EASTERN SIOUX VILLAGES
1800-1870
and battle sites , 1862-63 uprising

Key:
- △ Sioux villages
- ▢ Forts
- ⊺ Trading posts
- ● Agencies
- ✕ Battle sites
- ✝ Missions
- ■ 20th Century reservations

RIGHT **Little Crow, Mdewakanton, c1858.** A dynasty of chiefs from the Kapozha villages in Minnesota bore this name; this, the third, was the principal leader of the Santee Sioux uprising in Minnesota, 1862-63. After his defeat at Wood Lake he fled to the protection of his kinsmen on the Plains. Returning to his old haunts, he was killed on 3 July 1863 while picking berries near Hutchinson, Minnesota, by Nathan and Chauncey Lamson. His body was mutilated before burial, and Chauncey collected a bounty of $75 from the State for his scalp. Little Crow was probably nearly 60 years of age at the time of his death. Photograph by Joel E.Whitney. (Author's collection)

FAR RIGHT **John Other Day, Wahpeton.** Born in 1801, he became chief of the Wahpeton at Lac qui Parle, Minnesota. As a young man he was intemperate and fought against the Chippewa; later he became a Christian, and saved many white lives during the Inkpaduta (1857) and Minnesota (1862) outbreaks. Hostiles burned down his house in 1862, but the government later awarded him $2,500 for his bravery. He used it to buy a farm near Henderson, Minnesota, but later moved to the Sisseton/Wahpeton Reservation, South Dakota, where he died in 1871. (Photograph, author's collection)

bloods, so that when they were finally paid the annuities flowed into the hands of white traders. Further settler pressure in 1858 resulted in the northern strip of the reservation being ceded for additional cash and provisions. Winter 1861-62 brought near starvation to the Santee Sioux due to crop failure, and this was exacerbated by the failure of government clerks to distribute the Indians' cash and provisions in accordance with the treaty agreements.

Tension and demonstrations occurred at both agencies, and open conflict finally broke out after the killing of some white settlers near Acton by four Indians from the Lower Sioux Rice Creek village on 17 August 1862. A council of war followed. Wabasha, a foremost Lower Sioux chief, spoke against a war with the whites; but the opportunity offered by the draining of manpower from Minnesota by the American Civil War was urged by the Mdewakanton leader Little Crow, who encouraged an attack the following day on the Lower Agency, killing the hated trader Andrew Myrick. The refugees from the agency fled to Fort Ridgely; the Army retaliated, but were ambushed at the Redwood Ferry.

The Upper Agency Sioux were undecided about joining the war against the whites, and most actually took little active part, although they were often blamed for attacks and suffered as a consequence. John Other Day, an Upper Agency chief, was against the war and led several whites from the area to safety. Dr Stephen Riggs, a missionary to the Upper Sioux who translated the Bible into Dakota, was one who escaped from the Upper Agency.

The war continued as marauding Indians attacked white settlers and farmers over an ever-widening area, but the military at Fort Ridgely held firm despite two determined attacks by Sioux under Little Crow, Mankato and Big Eagle. Although some of the outbuildings were burned the fort's howitzers kept the Indians at bay. The siege was lifted on 27 August, thus securing the north bank of the Minnesota River from further incursions. **17**

Medicine Bottle, Eastern Sioux
warrior, 1864. Medicine Bottle,
or Wind-Rustling-Walker, and
Chief *Shakopee* ('Six'), two
Santee refugees in Canada after
the Minnesota uprising of 1862,
were befriended by US agents,
rendered helpless with alcohol
and chloroform, and spirited
back across the 'medicine line'
(border). They were subsequently
executed at Fort Snelling,
Minnesota, in November 1865.
Photograph by Whitney
& Zimmerman.
(Author's collection)

The Indian attacks on the south side were halted at the German town of New Ulm, whose volunteer forces were commanded by Charles Flandrau, although the town was evacuated on 25 August 1862.

After the successful defence of Fort Ridgely and New Ulm, organised military efforts to defeat and punish the Sioux began under Col Henry H.Sibley, a well-known fur trader, Minnesota Territory's first delegate to Congress, and the state's first governor. He arrived at Fort Ridgely with reinforcements, principally the 6th Minnesota Regiment. His first direction was for a burial party to leave Ridgely under Maj J.R.Brown and Capts J.Anderson and H.T.Grant; but they were attacked at Birch Coulee by Mankato warriors under Gray Bird, Red Legs and Big Eagle, who were probably diverted from their plans to attack white settlements down river. This event taught the whites the folly of moving in hostile country without a large, well-equipped force. In September the Sioux laid lengthy siege to Fort Abercrombie, but were eventually forced to withdraw. Following these actions the Sioux offensive ground to a halt.

The initiative now passed to Sibley and Flandrau, who were to implement the plan formulated by Governor Ramsey to free the many captives the Sioux held and then drive the hostiles out of Minnesota. After building up considerable forces at Ridgely, Sibley sent out offers of truce after receiving evidence of a division in the Indian ranks, and the peaceable Chief Wabasha arranged for the safe release of several white and mixed-blood captives. Sibley left Fort Ridgely with over 1,600 men including the interpreter Riggs and Other Day, who acted as scout. He encountered Little Crow at Wood Lake, and there followed a decisive victory for Sibley's forces which marked the end of organised warfare by the Sioux in Minnesota.

After the fighting at Wood Lake, Wabasha, Red Iron and the mixed-blood Gabriel Renville took control of the captives and more whites and mixed-bloods were released. About 1,200 Indians were taken into custody, increasing daily as individuals and small parties of Sioux, many facing starvation, surrendered. A military commission was appointed to try the Sioux at Camp Release and Lower Agency. As a result over 300 were sentenced to death, reduced to 39 due to the intervention of Bishop Henry B.Whipple of Faribault with President Lincoln; but 38 were hanged on 26 December 1862 at the town of Mankato. Those whose death sentences were commuted were later transferred from Mankato and imprisoned near Davenport, Iowa, for three years, while the uncondemned Sioux spent a miserable winter of 1862-63 in a fenced enclosure below Fort Snelling. In spring 1863 they were transported on river packets to Crow Creek in Dakota Territory, along with the Winnebagos who had been living near Mankato and who blamed their own removal on the Santee Sioux troubles. After three years of distress the Sioux were moved to the Santee Reservation near the mouth of the Niobrara River, Nebraska; and here these mostly Mdewakantons and Wahpekutes finally found a new home.

Absent from the punishment of the Sioux in 1862-63 was Little Crow himself, who after the Wood Lake battle had fled with others to the Dakota prairies – probably to Devil's Lake. In early 1863 he visited Fort Garry in Canada. He returned to Minnesota, however, and was killed on 3 July 1863. General Pope, who was convinced that the Upper and Lower Sioux now roaming the Dakota prairies could still be a menace to the Minnesota frontier, sent out two expeditions – one led by Sibley, which headed towards Devil's Lake, and the other by Sully from Fort Randall along the Missouri River. Sibley routed the Sioux at Big Mound and Stony Lake. Sully returned to the field in June 1864, and finally caught the Indians in the Killdeer Mountains of North Dakota, killing over a hundred of them. The expedition returned to Fort Ridgely in October after a march of 1,625 miles.

After 1866 Sioux raids on the Minnesota frontier gradually ceased, and the settlers and farmers slowly filtered back along the depopulated Minnesota River valley. Santees who had fled to the plains west of the river – mostly Sissetons and Wahpetons – were finally gathered on reservations in 1867, at Devil's Lake, North Dakota, and Sisseton or Lake Traverse, South Dakota. A principal leader of both bands between the death of Red Iron in 1884 and his own in 1892 was the mixed-blood Gabriel Renville. A few crossed into Canada and never returned, such as Standing Buffalo's band; but in the late 1860s small groups of Santees began to return to Minnesota, at Prairie Island, Red Wing, Prior Lake and at their old haunts at the Upper and Lower Agencies, where Chief Good Thunder – who had protected white settlers during the war – purchased lands in 1884. A few who left the Niobrara settled at Flandreau in 1869, where they succeeded as farmers and producers of catlinite pipes from the nearby Pipestone Quarry in Minnesota.

THE FINAL CONFLICT, 1870-90

Sioux history now returns to the West, where an uneasy peace held in 1870, although new leaders were emerging: Black Moon (Hunkpapa), Gall and Crazy Horse (Oglala), and a spiritual leader among the Hunkpapa – Sitting Bull. Red Cloud and Spotted Tail were now agency chiefs. Active hostilities resumed in 1871 during the survey for a railroad in an area still claimed by the Sioux. In 1872 there were Sioux attacks on the military at Pryor's Fork, Montana, and Fort Abraham Lincoln.

In 1873 rumours of gold in the Black Hills galvanised many hopeful whites into journeying west,

Delegation of Brulé Sioux to Washington, DC, from the Whetstone Agency under Capt Poole, May-June 1870: *(left to right)* Fast Bear, Spotted Tail, Swift Bear and Yellow Hair. Spotted Tail was born in about 1823; not a chief by birth, he rose to that rank by prowess in battle. He probably took part in the Grattan fight in August 1854 during depredations on the Oregon Trail. (Lt John Grattan was sent from Laramie to arrest a brave of Conquering Bear's Brulé band who had killed a Mormon's cow. In the resulting fight he and all but one of his men were killed by the Brulés, who had been joined by some Oglalas.) Spotted Tail was certainly present when Gen Harney took his revenge at Ash Hollow. He signed the 1868 Laramie Treaty; thereafter he was leader of the Brulés at the Rosebud Agency, near which he was murdered by Crow Dog in 1881. Today a college on the Rosebud Reservation perpetuates the old chief's name, *Sinte Gleska*. (Author's collection)

as they had earlier to the Californian and Montana goldfields. These prospectors broke the thin military cordon which had surrounded the Black Hills in accordance with the 1868 agreement. The government ordered a US Army expedition into the Black Hills. The chosen leader despatched to Fort Abraham Lincoln was the controversial LtCol George Armstrong Custer, commanding the US 7th Cavalry. He had a reputation as an Indian-hater who had butchered the Cheyennes (including Chief Black Kettle) on the Washita River, Oklahoma, on 27 November 1868.

The expedition of 1874 confirmed the presence of gold ore. The government concluded that it could only control the situation by prevailing on the Sioux to renegotiate the 1868 treaty and cede the Hills; they offered $6 million, but the Sioux refused. The military response was to withdraw troops from the approaches to the Black Hills, allowing miners to pour in. Some Sioux retaliated by killing miners and leaving the agencies for the remaining buffalo-hunting grounds to the west in the Yellowstone, Powder and Rosebud river country, outside the ring of forts which had encircled their lands.

The 1876 campaign

The US Army strategy for 1876 was to force these Sioux and their Cheyenne allies back to the agencies by encircling the Indians in south central Montana with three columns of troops: one under Col John Gibbon moving east from Fort Ellis at Bozeman, the second under Gen Alfred Terry (with Custer) moving west from Fort Abraham Lincoln near Bismarck, and the other under Gen George Crook moving north from Fort Fetterman on the North Platte. However, each column had only about 1,000 troops, some of dubious quality, who faced long marches to reach the area of the Rosebud, Tongue and Bighorn Rivers where the Indians were ranged. The plan received a major setback on 17 June on the Rosebud when Crook's 1,300-strong column was defeated by Crazy Horse, forcing him to withdraw to his base near present-day Sheridan, Wyoming; Crook took no further part in the campaign.

Terry and Gibbon met on the Yellowstone at the mouth of the Powder on 8 June, and conferred again on 21 June on the steamer *Far West* near the mouth of the Rosebud. Custer was despatched thence on 22 June, south down the Rosebud, with orders to swing north-west to the forks of the Bighorn and Little Bighorn, where Terry and Gibbon would be waiting. Custer tracked the pony hoofprints of the Indians west to a point now known as the Crow's Nest, a ridge about 15 miles from where a huge Indian village stretched along the Little Bighorn River. Custer's Arikara and Crow scouts reported the village early on 25 June, but they underestimated the numbers of hostiles in the vicinity.

Touch-the-Clouds, son of the Minneconjou patriarch Lone Horn who died on the Cheyenne River in 1875; he was born in 1836 and died in 1905. A legendary warrior, standing nearly seven feet tall, he was one of the Minneconjou chiefs at the battle of the Little Bighorn. He is seen here wearing the famous shirt worn by several Sioux chiefs for photographs, and which survives in the Buffalo Bill Historical Center, Cody, Wyoming (see page 45). Photograph by Julius Ulke, 1877.

Gall *(Pizi)*, Hunkpapa Sioux; born on the Moreau River, South Dakota, in 1840, he died at Oak Creek, South Dakota, in 1894. One of the principal military leaders at the Little Bighorn on 25 June 1876, he probably led the charge which finished Custer's command. He moved to Canada with Sitting Bull, but surrendered in Montana in 1881 and settled as a farmer on the Standing Rock Reservation, becoming a judge and a friend to the whites.

Although a recent examination of the Custer battlefield using modern forensic techniques has yielded new details, much basic information about this action remains unknown – including even Custer's exact route to his 'last stand'. The battle actually took place in the lands of the Crows, and the site is on the present-day Crow Reservation. Sitting Bull is known to have been present or nearby, and the following chiefs and bands took part: Hunkpapas under Gall and Black Moon, Oglalas under Crazy Horse, Minneconjous under Fast Bull, Sans Arcs under Fast Bear, Blackfoot under Scabby Head, Cheyennes under Two Moon and Ice Bear, Santees, Yanktons and Yanktonais under Inkpaduta.

Custer attacked at once, dividing his 7th Cavalry into three parties. Captain Frederick Benteen, with Companies D, H and K, was sent south to scout and report Indian movements; Maj Marcus A.Reno led Cos. A, M and G against the southern edge of the village. Custer himself would advance northwards with Cos. C, E, F, L and I, some say following the line of a ridge running parallel to the village, which was scattered along the wooded valley to his left on the west bank of the Little Bighorn River. He then apparently swung west over the crest of the ridge, intending to cross the river and attack the northern end of the village. All we really know of the Custer attack is from Indian accounts recorded much later, and these are often confused. At what point he crossed the ridge or even if he ever reached the river remains in dispute. His column was certainly repulsed and cut to pieces, some succeeding in retreating to a rise since named Custer Hill, where a monument now stands. Custer was outnumbered and totally overwhelmed by fresh and probably better-armed warriors frantic to defend their women and children.

With him died 214 men, including his brothers Tom and Boston, a nephew and a brother-in-law. Mutilated corpses were found in four groups strewn on Calhoun Ridge, and another about half a mile north. Some 40 men had fallen with Custer on the hill which bears his name, and about 30 bodies were found near the river in a ravine. To the south, Maj Reno hit the village but halted his charge when confronted by an enormous number of warriors; he formed a skirmish line, from which he later retreated across the river, to be rejoined by Benteen's battalion, ultimately on a site now known as Reno Hill. Here fighting continued until 26 June; no serious attempt was made to break out of this defensive position, although a few made brave dashes to reach water, and one of Benteen's officers, Thomas B.Weir, moved to a vantage point from where his troops caught glimpses of the Indians through the smoke of battle to the north. After losing 47 killed, Reno was relieved by Terry on the 26th, shortly after the great Indian camp had broken up, setting fire to the grass – the Indians knew retribution was bound to follow.

During the high summer and autumn of 1876 Crook returned to the field, where his subordinates Col Wesley Merritt (5th Cavalry) and Capt Anson Mills (3rd Cavalry) gained victories over the Sioux at Warbonnet Creek, Nebraska, and Slim Buttes, South Dakota, respectively; in the latter fight Chief American Horse was killed. In October Col Nelson Miles held a meeting with Sitting Bull which ended in a running battle. During the following winter Cols Miles and Mackenzie (4th Cavalry) harassed the Cheyennes and Sioux, until by May 1877 most had returned and surrendered to the agencies.

However, the flow of fortune-hunters into the Black Hills did not diminish despite the fighting. Another government commission was charged with the task of obtaining the Black Hills by a treaty change to the western boundary of The Great Sioux Reservation. Although the agency chiefs Red Cloud, Red Leaf, Spotted Tail and John Grass signed, many did not; but the articles of the agreement were passed by Congress in February 1877. Sitting Bull crossed into Canada with High Bear and Gall, but Crazy Horse and his Oglalas and Cheyennes were defeated by Col Mackenzie; Crazy Horse surrendered in the spring of 1877, and was imprisoned and murdered. Gall and Sitting Bull returned to the Standing Rock Agency in 1881. *(continued on page 24)*

Sioux beliefs

The Sioux believed that all natural and cultural phenomena could be transformed; those permanently transformed are collectively *Wakantanka*, glossed as 'Great Spirit', 'Great Mystery' or 'God' – but have a collective meaning. Man is considered powerless when confronted by nature, and cries out for pity when help is required. He addresses Wakantanka in the metaphor of kinship, Father or Grandfather. Those who are answered or transformed are *Wakan* (holy). Wakantanka has aspects of fours: four times four or four times seven, i.e. four seasons, four phases of the moon, four directions. The energy of the universe can be controlled by Wakantanka or *Wakansica* (evil sacred); man is subordinate to both. There are 16 aspects of Wakantanka in groups of four in descending importance: Sun, Sky, Earth and Rock; Moon, Wind, Falling Stars, Thunder Being; Buffalo, Two-legged (Bear or Man), Four Winds, Whirlwind; Shade, Breath, Shade-like and Potency. In addition there are other supernatural beings, some benevolent and some malevolent: Spider, Old Man, Wizard and Old Woman.

Those who mediate between supernatural beings and powers and ordinary people are glossed as 'holy' men or women (Wakan people), who can be distinguished from those who administer herbal medicine, *Pejuta Wicasa*, glossed as 'medicine man'. The Wakan people received visions to intercede for good hunting, predicted the outcome of war parties, found lost objects, and were interpreters of sacred myths and directors of ceremonials.

Dream societies were formed by men who received the same or similar visions of an animal. The Heyoka Society received visions of Thunder Beings; it was required that members acted opposite to normal, e.g. dressed heavily in summer, scantily in winter, spoke backwards or acted as clowns. The Elk Dreamers were imbued with special powers over women. Other animal cults were Bear, Black-tailed Deer, Wolf, Buffalo, Mountain Sheep; there were also a Berdache Cult and Double(-faced) Woman Cult with the power to seduce men.

Holy people were separate from ordinary people by their ability not only to interpret a sacred knowledge but to share this knowledge with the supernatural and other holy people by means of a sacred language. The legend of the coming of the White Buffalo Calf Woman to the Sans Arc band probably coincides with the reformation of Teton religion, which seems to have occurred about the same time as the Teton were increasing in numbers and power in about 1800. She gave directions for a number of rites to influence the supernatural beings to a band of Sans Arc under Standing Buffalo, after meeting two of his scouts out looking for buffalo. She presented a sacred calf pipe bundle to them, directing them in the use of the sacred pipe in the rituals. It is believed that the bundle (or a form of it) still exists amongst Sans Arc descendants on the Cheyenne River Reservation, South Dakota, to this day. She gave instructions for various rituals, briefly as follows:

(1) The Adoption rite or The Making of Relatives – *Hunkalowanpi*, or simply *Hunka*. Its purpose was to bond men together ceremonially, involving the use of special wands often decorated with feathers and horsetails.

(2) Sun Dance – *Wiwayankwacipi*. A calendrical ceremony during the early summer when several bands were together for a common buffalo hunt, undertaken to fulfil the vows of various men by praying for the tribal well-being. The ceremonial is performed in a large lodge of posts and rafters with brush to form areas of shade. The rafters adjoin a centre pole which was 'captured' by warriors (regarded as enemy), erected vertically in a hole around which the lodge is completed, usually about 25 yards in diameter. Within the lodge rituals are performed over a number of days (see below – also Plate B).

(3) Vision Quest – *Hanbleceyapi*. Usually performed during adolescence to seek a vision or to gain power.

(4) Spirit-Keepers or Ghost Keeping – *Wakicagapi*. The spirit of the deceased was 'kept' ritually before travelling south to the Milky Way, sometimes for up to two years before the soul was released.

(5) Throwing of the Ball – *Tapawankayeyapi*. Based on the legend of a buffalo calf who grew into a woman who had a ball made which symbolically represented the universe and was used in ritual games.

(6) Girls' Puberty Ritual, also known as the Buffalo Rite – *atankalowanpi*. During the buffalo supernatural's guard

over a pubescent girl, which established her relationship to the sacred White Buffalo Calf Woman.

(7) The Sweat Lodge, the Rite of Purification – *Inipi*. Communal purification in a heated sweat lodge, a small circular dome-shaped lodge with hot stones (see Plate B).

Winter counts tend to confirm that the White Buffalo Calf Woman legend dates from about 1797-98, so we can conclude that these ceremonials are of no great age, perhaps late enough to have been influenced by white missionaries.

The **Sun Dance** was the most important ceremony of the Plains Indians; the name is misleading, although the male dancers do gaze towards the rising morning sun. Its purpose was a world re-creation or renewal rite, and it followed the vows of those who had received visionary commands to sponsor a dance. After the lodge was built the skull of a buffalo or buffalo and human cut-out effigies and other offerings were fixed to the centre pole. The public phase of the ritual saw the formal procession of barefooted dancers into the lodge, gazing at the centre pole or Sun, blowing their eagle-bone whistles, bending their knives at the beat of a drum. They kept dancing for several days and nights, hoping for a vision or to arouse the pity of Wakantanka. Finally – amongst the Teton – several participants who had vowed to do so would have themselves pierced through the pectoral muscles by skewers by means of which they would be tethered to the centre pole. They would dance back and forth, attempting to tear themselves free, to gain supernatural aid through their ecstasy of pain and the pity of Wakantanka.

Although the Sun Dance was banned in 1881, after 1934 it was officially reinstated and attenuated versions are still performed, despite attempts by non-traditionalists to commercialise the ritual in the 1960s. Only the girls' puberty ritual and Throwing of the Ball game are no longer performed; the other rites survive amongst a few traditionalists.

An important night cult amongst the Teton was *Yuwipi*, which survives amongst traditionalist Indians, for curing sickness, finding lost objects or missing persons, predicting future events, giving advice and offering protection. The cult appears to be a variant of the Shaking Tipi Rite of the northern Indians (Ojibwa and Cree), used for aid in hunting, whereby spirits were induced to search for moose and deer.

OPPOSITE **Santee Sioux Grass Dancers photographed at Fort Totten, North Dakota, c1900. Note the 'hairpipe' breastplate (right), massive necklaces (centre/left), mirror board (right), and the pipe-tomahawk held by the central dancer. The Santee generally had narrower heads than the Teton, clearly shown in this photograph.**

RIGHT **Sitting Bull, Hunkpapa, 1884. This tribal leader and holy man, born on the Grand River, South Dakota, in 1834, took an active part in the Plains wars of the 1860s, including a raid on Fort Buford in 1866. A member of the Strong Hearts warrior society, he presided at a Sun Dance on the Rosebud River in mid-June 1876 and had a vision of soldiers falling into his camp, which was taken as a prediction of the forthcoming battle on the Little Bighorn**

a few days later. His presence in the Rosebud country attracted many warriors who took part in the defeat of Custer's command. He fled to Canada and joined Black Moon, but surrendered at Fort Buford in 1881, and was confined at Fort Randall until 1883. He then settled at Standing Rock Agency, but was killed by Indian police during Ghost Dance disturbances in 1890. A few descendants of Sitting Bull's band who remained in Saskatchewan, Canada, still live near Wood Mountain. He is seen here wearing a buckskin jacket with floral beaded designs, holding a tobacco bag and pipe. Photograph by Palmquist & Jurgens.

The decade of the 1880s was a traumatic time for the Western Sioux. The Great Sioux Reservation – all of present-day South Dakota west of the Missouri River – had been set aside for the seven western Sioux bands by the treaty of 1868. It was reduced in size by the Black Hills cession of 1877, and again in 1889 when the Sioux surrendered nine million acres and were forced to accept six separate reservations in place of the single large one. Using the control of rations the Indian agents sought to destroy the old Indian social and religious customs, including discouraging Indian dress and hairstyles. The nomadic warrior-hunter culture had gone, and the Sioux were to become farmers, ranchers and Christians; many were dependent upon agency rations for food, as the last of the buffalo had gone by 1884. The Sioux were no longer in control of their own destiny.

In 1889 the Sioux heard of a new cult which derived from earlier forms amongst the Paiute Indians of Nevada. Sioux pilgrims visited the cult leader Wovoka at Walker River, and on their return described him as Messiah, having returned from heaven with a message of peace and reconciliation. The Sioux, however, added their own interpretations: a new earth, the return of the buffalo, and the belief that wearing ritual clothes painted with symbols would protect the wearer if shot by white soldiers. The Ghost Dance rituals – so-called because it was claimed that the ghosts of ancestors would return – aroused great excitement on the

Teton social organisation

Each of the Teton bands (or 'hoops') was further divided into smaller bands known as *tiyospaye* or 'camps', each led by chiefs called *itancan*, with political power vested in the 'Chiefs' Society' of seven foremost leaders – *wicasa itancan*, 'Chief Man'. These tiyospaye consisted of extended and continually changing bilateral and bi-local kin groups called *wicoti*.

Teton political life began at the beginning of each summer, when bands unable to live together during the winter because of lack of game convened in a huge encampment of tipis pitched in the form of a large circle (sacred hoop) with an opening (door) on the east side. Smaller bands were assigned certain places; the favourite was at the entrance (horn) opposite the tipi of the head chief. The council lodge was pitched in an open space at the centre of the hoop.

The overall picture of well-developed social and military societies with elaborate initiation ceremonies and other rites, a complex order of chieftaincy with gradations in rank and defined roles, and institutions such as councils and *akicita* (camp policemen, who assumed a great deal of authority) is probably inaccurate. The political and ceremonial associations of the Teton were established so late, and flowered so quickly – as a result of the horse-rich economy, trading links, and offensive warfare – that perhaps only during the observance of major ceremonies such as the Sun Dance did such organisations function successfully. The rise in population after the acquisition of the horse, through attracting eastern bands to the Teton and particularly to the Oglala,

resulted in shifting loyalties and self-made band chiefs; others were hereditary figures who displayed leadership qualities. Violent attacks between band members, selfishness, and even tyranny were only sometimes tempered by conspicuous generosity. Amongst the Oglala, a schism opened in 1841 following a confrontation between chiefs Bull Bear and Smoke and really never healed. The Oglala council or chiefs' society *Tezi Tanka* ('Big Bellies', i.e. men over 40) delegated authority to four younger men, so-called 'Shirt Wearers' (from their badge of office); they also appointed others who determined where camps would be located and hunting permitted.

The decisions were carried out by akicita, members of warrior or soldier societies noted amongst all Sioux groups including the Santee. The akicita 'soldiers' were members of various age-graded warrior societies such as the Kit Foxes, Crow Owners (referring to a special type of feather dance bustle), Badgers, Bare Lance Owners, Owl Feather Headdress, White Horse Riders, and Strong Hearts (famous for their unique ermine-decorated horned bonnets, worn only in battle). The Silent Eaters, of which Sitting Bull was a member, were another version of the Big Bellies confined to the Hunkpapas. The societies which were designed as fighting groups each fought as a unit whenever possible, and each had its own chief, heralds or criers, and coterie of four virtuous young women. In 1878-79 when the Oglalas were moved to Pine Ridge Agency the seven tiyospaye located in various parts of the agency formed some conservative Indian communities which survive to the present day.

5: Yanktonai Sioux earth lodge

COSTUME, c1825-50
1: Teton Sioux man, c1850
2: Teton Sioux woman and child, c1830
3: Yanktonai Sioux man, c1830

4: Santee Sioux girl, c1825

A

1 & 2

3

4

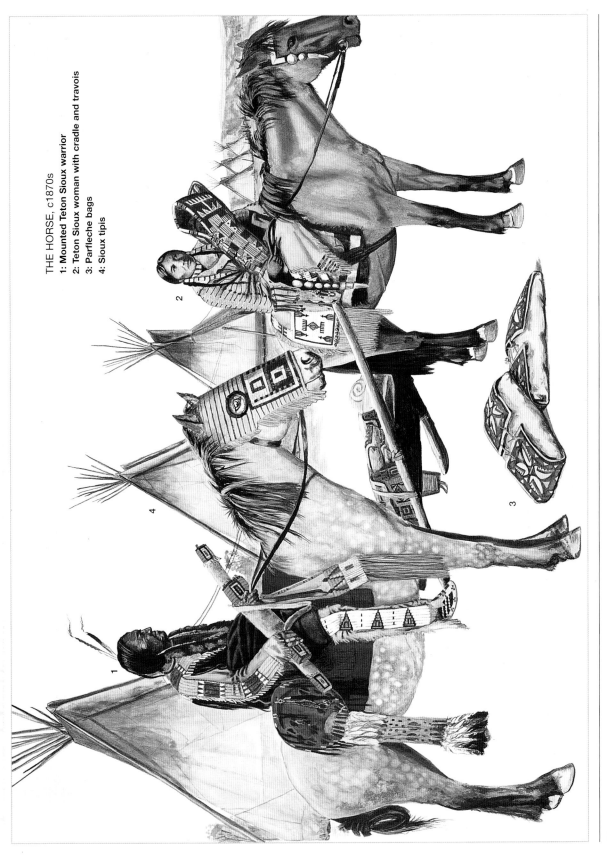

THE HORSE, c1870s
1: Mounted Teton Sioux warrior
2: Teton Sioux woman with cradle and travois
3: Parfleche bags
4: Sioux tipis

C

MALE COSTUME, c1860-90
1: Teton Sioux man, c1890
2: Yanktonai Sioux man, c1875
3: Santee Sioux man, 1860s
4: Teton Sioux boy, c1885

D

FEMALE COSTUME, c1870-90
1: Teton Sioux woman, 1870
3: Yanktonai Sioux woman, 1880
4: Teton Sioux girl, 1890
2: Santee Sioux woman, 1860-80
5: Santee Sioux bark lodge

E

WARRIOR SOCIETIES
1: Omaha Society, c1890
2: Miwatani or Mandan Society, c1870
3: Strong Heart Society, c1880
4: Fox or Kit Fox Society, c1880

F

THE RESERVATIONS
1: Sioux male Ghost Dancer, c1890
2: Sioux female Ghost Dancer, c1890
3: Sioux boy, c1890
4: Sioux baby girl, c1890
5: Teton Sioux man and woman, c1907

G

CONTEMPORARY POWWOW COSTUME

1: Contemporary male dancer, c1988
2: Flag bearer, c1980
3: Contemporary male dancer, c1995

Sioux agencies in 1890, both amongst the Indian converts and the military. The agent at Standing Rock, James McLaughlin, ordered the Indian police to restrict Sitting Bull, whose ardent followers had been Ghost Dancing for weeks. In the confrontation which followed outside Sitting Bull's cabin on 15 December 1890 the chief was shot dead by Red Tomahawk, an Indian policeman.

A band of Ghost Dancers from Cheyenne River under Big Foot, heading south for the Bad Lands presumably to join Kicking Bear and Short Bull, was intercepted by Maj Whitside and escorted to Wounded Knee Creek on the Pine Ridge Reservation. By a twist of fate the troops who now held Big Foot's band were from the 7th Cavalry, cut to pieces on the Little Bighorn 14 years earlier. On 29 December 1890 the soldiers, now under the command of Col Forsyth, surrounded the Indian camp; and during the confrontation that followed soldiers using rifles and howitzers killed 300 men, women and children. The dead were buried in a common grave, which remains today a memorial to the long sufferings of the Sioux people over the past three and a half centuries.

THE AFTERMATH, 1890-1990

The Dawes Act of 1887 disposed of more Sioux territory by the passing of 'excess' (unoccupied) lands on The Great Sioux Reservation to whites. This process did not stop until the 1934 Indian Reorganisation Act, which allowed self-governing tribal councils on each reservation to handle internal affairs. Such councils inevitably fell under the control of acculturated mixed-bloods, leading to factionalism between them and traditionalists. By 1900 the Eastern Sioux were largely living like 'poor whites', often as farmers. A large proportion of them were of mixed blood, having intermarried with fur traders – mostly French – since the mid-18th century. The Western Sioux had partly intermarried with the Missouri River traders during the 19th century, and 1,000 mixed-bloods were settled at the Whetstone Agency alone by around 1870. Conditions on the Western Sioux reservations were, and often still are, characterised by poverty. By 1890 log cabins were replacing tipis, food including beef was distributed by the Indian agencies, but diet was poor, resulting in widespread ill-health. Most Indians joined Christian denominations, and Indian dress and native practices were discouraged or actually banned by government officials. However, native language and religion survived amongst the predominantly full-blood *tiyospaye* communities such as those at Pine Ridge.

Reservation populations have evolved into a number of social groups divided by economics, religion, social achievement and blood quantum. During the first half of the 20th century many Western Sioux retained their skills in horsemanship, becoming 'cowboys' as western culture

Curley, the famous Crow scout who brought the news of Custer's defeat to the US Army headquarters on the steamer *Far West*, thereafter becoming something of a celebrity. Here he wears a loop necklace, and holds a shield trimmed with eagle feathers. Unknown photographer, c1900. (Photograph, author's collection)

ABOVE **American Horse, Oglala. Probably the son or nephew of the American Horse killed by Captain Anson Mill's 3rd Cavalry detatchment at Slim Buttes, South Dakota, on 29 September 1876 following the battle of the Little Bighorn. This American Horse signed the treaty in 1887 by which The Great Sioux Reservation was reduced by approximately one half. He visited Washington on several occasions, and in 1891 obtained a commitment to fairer ration distribution at the agencies. (Postcard, author's collection)**

integrated with tribal life. Young Sioux men served in the US armed forces in both World Wars and the Korean and Vietnam conflicts. In 1973 the American Indian Movement (AIM), initially founded in the cities by acculturated and college-educated Métis of many tribes, was successful in bringing to the attention of the general public the wrongs perpetrated against the Native American by US government policies over many years. In a confrontation with the Bureau of Indian Affairs at Wounded Knee, site of the massacre of 1890, two people were killed during a stand-off which has become a symbolic statement of continued Federal injustices to all American Indians.

The economic situation on many reservations is still very depressed; people still receive commodities from the Federal government, and health conditions generally fall below average national levels. Today, however, the Sioux promote special classes for their language, arts, music and dance, and colleges have been established at Pine Ridge, Rosebud and Standing Rock, one of which has received university status. Indian culture survives in revived Sun Dances (somewhat shortened versions), vision quests, sweat lodges, memorial feasts, wakes and Yuwipis. The Pan-Indian powwows are popular on all reservations, with changing forms of social dance costume and songs, and prizes for the best performers in various categories. A revival in craftwork augments the powwow scene. On the downside, the regular use of native language by the younger generations is rapidly decreasing; it will probably not survive long into the 21st century as a first language, and is already almost wholly lost amongst the Santee. Unfortunately, problems with alcohol still abound, causing family breakdown; and average family incomes are far below national levels.

Kicking Bear and Short Bull, Minneconjou and Brulé Sioux, leaders of the Ghost Dance cult who brought the religion from the Paiute in Nevada to the Sioux reservations. Photograph by John Grabill, 1891. (Postcard, author's collection)

Material culture and dress

Santee

During summer the Santee lived in large wooden pitched-roof lodges -'House-big'- with sleeping platforms inside; in winter small wigwams of bark or cattail mats were used. Some western Santees, closer to the High Plains, used the tipi. It is likely that the Santee at one time used bark canoes, but only dug-outs were noted by white traders after they had moved from their original forest homeland to the prairies where bark was scarce. Food was derived from hunting, fishing, gathering and horticulture. They collected wild rice, maple sugar and wild turnips and grew corn, beans, squash, pumpkin and tobacco.

Their **dress** more closely resembled Algonkian and Siouan neighbours to the east and south than their own kinsmen to the west. Santee headmen wore buckskin shirts of two skins (deer, elk, antelope) similar to those of the Yanktonai to the west, somewhat more close fitting than those of the Teton, with quilled strips (sometimes of bird quills) along the arms and shoulders. Later cloth shirts decorated with beadwork were used. Leggings were sometimes buckskin, tightly fitting, with a seam at the front, held by a belt and by garters at the knee. Santee women wore the two-piece dress, consisting of a wrap-around skirt ornamented with ribbonwork and a loose-fitting blouse with silver brooches or beadwork after the appearance of white traders. Moccasins were soft-soled, originally with a single seam over the instep, with ankle flaps; later a style with a vamp was adopted.

Santees were frequent visitors to Fort Garry and the Métis settlements in Manitoba during the 19th century, and no doubt adopted from them one form of floral beadwork after glass beads became plentiful from white traders. Another beadwork style resembled Chippewa work; yet another, the large stylised floral forms of the Winnebago, who lived in close association with the Santee during the 19th century.

Bows were long, about 3½ feet. For close fighting clubs were used, both the ball-headed type known and used by all the eastern tribes and the 'gun-stock' warclub. The explorer Jonathan Carver reported in the 18th century that Santee men also wore a triangular chest-piece sheath with a dagger, as shown in the oldest known sketch of a Sioux Indian. Santee warriors usually went into battle naked except for breechcloth, leggings and moccasins, preferring ambush tactics to open warfare. The highest acclaim for warriors was to touch an enemy (counting coup), a trait shared with all Sioux divisions. Success in warfare required the use of war bundles, and was celebrated with victory and scalp dances.

Burial was either in the ground with a small wooden house built over the grave, or corpses were placed on raised scaffolds or in trees, the latter a custom shared with the Western Sioux. The **ceremonial** life of the Santee was derived from both Woodland and High Plains cultures, as their intermediate geographical position would indicate. From Woodland sources came Vision

Mr & Mrs Blackshield, Santee Sioux, at Fort Totten (Devil's Lake) Reservation, c1910. Note the floral beaded bandolier bags worn by the man, of a style usually associated with the Ojibwa. They were worn by the Santee on ceremonial occasions, and probably made by them. (Photograph courtesy Alvina Alberts & Louis Garcia)

Quest, Medicine Feast, Adoption Feast, and Medecine Lodge – a graded curative society similar to that of the Ojibwa. From High Plains influences came the Sun Dance (used by some groups), Horse Dance, Warrior Society dances and the Grass Dance. The latter, after shedding some of its original religious associations, was carried to Canada where a newer form evolved to become a Pan-Indian movement, the northern Grass Dance. The Santee transmitted the older form to their eastern neighbours in the 19th century.

Yankton

The Yankton and Yanktonai, together forming the Yankton division of the Sioux, used both the skin tipi and the earth lodge, although probably only the Yanktonai built earth lodges similar to those associated with the Mandan and Hidatsa. Bullboats, a type of coracle similar to those of the Mandan, were also used. The economy of these middle branches of the Sioux resembled other Missouri River groups, being based upon hunting, gathering and river-bottom horticulture. Great tribal bison hunts took place twice a year, in mid-summer and fall. Fishing was not so important as it was to the Santee, but the gathering of turnips, chokecherries and other wild foods was important. As with the Teton, government was by chief and council assisted by akicita members or soldiers. Chieftainship tended to be hereditary.

Men wore hair-fringed **buckskin shirts** with porcupine-quilled strips over the shoulders and along the arms similar to the northern Teton (Saone), with square or triangular neck flaps. Leggings were originally buckskin with quilled strips, or later of trade cloth with a box design of a contrasting material. Women wore the classic two-skin hide dress, in later times extended with a yoke or cape to become a three-skin dress similar to those of the Teton, the cape covered with dentalium

(continued overleaf)

shells or, after their introduction, with small glass beads. Women also wore vertically strung traded bone 'hairpipes', again similar to Teton women. Cradles resembled the Plains type, unlike the cradleboards of the Santee.

Shields were made from the neck of a bull bison, treated by a process of heating and shrinking until convex and half-an-inch thick, and painted with protective designs. The Middle Sioux employed the short bow adapted for use on horseback, and stone-headed war clubs of the High Plains type. During the mid- to late 19th century they developed beadwork which was geometrical in design, but floral work was adopted from their eastern neighbours. Men often wore fur turbans and huge grizzly bear claw necklaces, or later loop necklaces. In later years leading men wore eagle feather **'warbonnets'**, and the young men wore the costume associated with the northern Grass Dance. The Sun Dance was the most important religious ceremony, and shamans with 'bear power' were skilled with herbal medicines. The Yanktonai were at the centre of a trade system which connected the Sioux with British, American and other native goods, resulting in a mixed material culture from the late 18th century.

Teton

The conical buffalo (bison) skin **tipi** or lodge was the universal dwelling of the nomadic Teton after crossing the Missouri River into the High Plains during the mid-18th century (see Plate C4). In the early decades of the reservation period tipis were largely replaced by log cabins or government buildings, although tipis were still erected for special occasions or used as summer homes, though now made out of canvas duck of Army issue. White canvas tipi lodges can still be seen at modern Indian gatherings and are still sometimes used for Peyote and Yuwipi meetings. Large tipi covers and household belongings could be transported easily and quickly by travois, a platform mounted on a frame of poles dragged behind a horse. Rawhide parfleche cases decorated with painted geometrical designs were used to store clothes and meat.

Most male and female **clothing** was originally made from untailored deer or antelope hides prepared by women. Bison robes with hair left on one side, painted on the other with warrior scenes and feather circle designs, were worn by men; women wore robes painted with symbolic designs in so-called 'box-and-border' styles. Authorities have disagreed on the interpretation of symbolism in much of Plains Indian art, which quickly lost its function during the dramatic changes of the second half of the 19th century. Bison robes were replaced by blankets, and selvedge-edged wool trade cloth with beaded strips added was popular in the late 19th century.

Certainly the spread of and ultimate dependence on fur trade goods can be considered as an east-to-west advance, the Teton being the last to become associated with white traders. (The Santee, when first visually recorded by visiting government officials in the early 19th century, had already adopted European dress. Both

Medicine Bear (Mato-wakan), Upper Yanktonai Sioux chief, 1872. He is wearing a fur headdress, bear claw necklace, and buckskin shirt with quillwork strips; and holds a decorated pipe, with a feather fan in the crook of his arm. Photograph by Alexander Gardner.

male and female dress consisted of traded cloth, printed cotton blouses, shirts of broadcloth, and chiefs' coats – special coats distributed by traders. However, for ceremonials and treaty gatherings chiefs reverted to skin shirts and leggings resembling those of their western cousins, although more tailored.)

The **bison**, essential to Plains Indian life, supplied the Sioux with the materials for tipis, glue, rope, fuel, household implements, tools, bladder pouches, shields and food. From elk antler and horn were fashioned hide-scrapers, spoons and dippers. Bison meat was cut in long strips and hung up to dry; some was pounded and mixed with crushed berries to make into pemmican which could be stored for winter.

The Sioux kept **records** of important happenings in their tribal or personal history by means of so-called 'winter counts', *Waniyetu Wowapi*. These were records of the events of each 'winter', painted on hide (or later on canvas or muslin), which became calendrical chronicles of events stretching back many generations.

Horses became integrated into Sioux life from about 1750. In the warrior society, based on individual prestige gained through war, raiding for horses was one of the primary causes of intertribal clashes, as horses were a symbol of a man's wealth. Warriors decorated horses with eagle feathers or painted their flanks with designs to lend them speed and courage. Women's wooden saddles and stirrups were of a type derived from a Spanish (or perhaps ultimately, Moorish) style. Men rode bare-backed or used pad-saddles (traded from the north) or saddle blankets, and kept control with horsehair bridles; their horses were bedecked with face masks and headstalls for ceremonials and celebrations.

Smoking customs involving the spiritual use of pipes, or originally so-called 'calumets' with feather heraldry, were certainly pre-European and possibly 'Mississippian' (a prehistoric farming culture) in origin. The pipeheads were often made of a steatite called 'catlinite' (a red stone from a quarry in present-day Minnesota), and the stems were of carved ash decorated with quillwork or beadwork.

The most popular **weapons** for close fighting were stone clubs with long wooden handles. The stone head was grooved around the centre to take a rawhide band which was bound to the handle with sinew. The handle was then covered with buckskin sewn with heavy sinew and sometimes decorated with beadwork and a pendant of bison- or horsehair. Other so-called 'slung-shot' clubs had buckskin-encased stone heads at the end of buckskin-covered wooden handles. Later ornamental clubs had handles inserted in drilled stone heads. The Santee used gunstock-shaped clubs with traded metal blades, and iron axes and pipe-tomahawks became available through the English fur trade from the 18th century onwards. Bows were made of hardwoods – yew, ash, hickory – 3ft to 4ft long, sometimes painted, or decorated with brass tacks, beads or red trade cloth. Arrows with triple fletchings of hawk feathers, with inserted stone or, later, metal points, were carried with the bow in combined quivers and bowcases of buckskin. Traded percussion rifles were common by 1820. Shields were made from thick bison hide and painted with protective designs, and were sometimes kept in a secondary cover.

Horizontally-strung 'hairpipe breastplates' were very popular amongst Sioux men and vertically-strung ones amongst their women. The manufacture of commercially made shell **hairpipes** began in the 18th century, perhaps to replace Wampum, silver and brass ornaments in the eastern Indian trade. The term 'hairpipe' probably refers to their early use as hair ornaments. Their manufacture began amongst the Dutch settlers in New Jersey who sold them to the great trading companies, who in turn sold them to groups involved in the Indian fur trade. The Western Sioux got their first shell hairpipes in about 1800, along with trade silver arm bands, gorgets, brooches, ear wheels, finger rings and ear bobs. In the early 19th century hairpipes were used to make necklaces,

chokers and hair ornaments, and it was probably the Comanche who invented the hairpipe breastplate by stringing them horizontally on buckskin cords. The earliest photographs of Western Sioux men wearing hairpipe breastplates are among those taken in Washington in 1872 during a visit by Sioux leaders, although they had earlier made dentalium shell necklaces, ear ornaments and breastplates. In about 1880, as the demand for large numbers of hairpipes for use in making elaborate breastplates was increasing, the Sioux began to obtain a cheaper and less fragile type made of cattle bone. The Sioux used bone hairpipe breastplates of two or three rows wide, each about 4in to 4½ins long, extending to the waist, usually spaced between rawhide strips and brass beads. Hairpipes are still used today, although usually of composite materials. Women strung the hairpipes vertically into complex necklaces reaching almost to their knees.

Sioux **moccasins** were probably originally of the single-piece side seam or centre seam type used by the Santee, which reflect a Woodland/Prairie form. However, the Western Sioux developed moccasins with separate, hard soles in about 1840 – probably due to European influence – and these proved sturdier for High Plains terrain. Moccasins were quilled or beaded with geometrical designs.

Cradles were made in the form of rectangular hide bags, fastened with buckskin thongs at the front and heavily beaded. A variant with a beaded cradle hood and supporting wood lattice frame, more usually associated with the Cheyenne, was also sometimes used by the Sioux. The Eastern Sioux used a cradle made from a wooden board fitted with a protective bow for the child's

(continued overleaf)

Afraid-of-Hawk, Oglala band, Teton Sioux, 1898. He holds a typical stone-headed club, the handle decorated with beadwork. He wears in his hair a quilled 'circle of the world' with a trailer of beads (probably brass) and eagle feathers attached. Probably photographed by Heyn during the Trans-Mississippi Exposition at Omaha, Nebraska. (Author's collection)

head and a place to hang trinkets – a style they shared with the Pawnee, Oto and Osage; the baby was wrapped and held against the board.

The Eastern Sioux began to obtain European trade goods well before the turn of the 18th century, but it was not until the early 1800s that the Western Sioux became involved in the fur trade and received trade goods in exchange. By 1850 great changes were taking place in Sioux art and design. Porcupine quillwork and painted designs had been the principal means of artistic decoration of religious objects and ceremonial dress. Flattened quills were dyed with natural pigments, plaited, and sewn down in lanes with sinew thread to produce areas of solid quillwork in simple geometrical patterns. Sometimes bird quills or maidenhair fern were also used.

The first European **beads** obtained by the Teton and some branches of the Santee, Yanktonai and Yankton for embroidery were so-called 'pony beads', usually blue, red and white, and quill designs were adapted for these earliest beadwork elements. Earlier only large necklace trade beads had been used. Pony beads have been so named because they were carried by the traders' ponies in back packs. Shells, mostly dentalium shells, were also brought to the Plains by traders, and the Sioux used them for earrings and chokers.

From about 1860 huge quantities of glass 'seed beads' in a wide range of colours became increasingly available, produced in Venice and Bohemia. These allowed the transformation of Sioux decorative art and design from simple squares, rectangles and triangles to highly complex geometrical shapes. Some art historians believe this was an indigenous development using new materials; others, that it was influenced by designs on imported multi-patterned Middle Eastern rugs and carpets or copies seen at Army posts or traders' stores.

Beadwork ultimately covered moccasins, dress yokes and storage bags and was used on shirts, leggings, tobacco bags, horsegear and weapons.

Tetons became the most prolific beadworkers on the Plains, possibly because the new way of life on the reservations afforded women more spare time. Their technique of beading is called 'lazy stitch': eight to ten beads are strung on sinew into a row, stitched only at the ends, and built up to cover large areas in lanes.

The Western Sioux continued to dress in their Indian clothes for **tribal gatherings** and Fourth of July celebrations long after white man's clothes were commonplace for everyday wear. These social gatherings were an outward display of continuing Indian life acceptable to the white agency officials and missionaries who had driven native religion and ritual underground. (Even in displays of the Grass Dance in specially constructed dance halls men were required to don 'long john' underclothes under their regalia.) The Grass Dance became so popular – displacing society dances of a more religious type, yet incorporating features of old warrior rituals – that it has become the basis of the modern Indian powwow. The northern form (Canadian Grass Dance), the Sioux form (sometimes called the Omaha Dance), and the southern form (the Hethuska) all descend from the old Omaha-Ponca prototype.

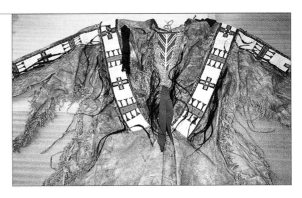

A Teton Sioux shirt, now in the collection of University of Cambridge, UK, Museum of Archaeology and Anthropology, Acc.No.219215 – an earlier assession number (3312) suggests a transfer from another museum, probably an exchange with either the old Heye Foundation in New York or the Smithsonian Institution, Washington, DC. The style and decoration appear to be typically Teton Sioux and probably either Oglala or Brulé, made some time between 1885 and 1895. Despite its fairly late date, suggested by the use of metal beads, it retains much of the important Teton symbolism of older shirts such as those worn by delegates of the Oglala chiefs' society.

The shirt is constructed with two large deer or elk skins forming the front and back and smaller skins forming the arms, with extensions under the arms added to resemble the older untailored shirts of the early 19th century. The colour symbolism is old: an upper area painted blue (here a greenish-blue shade), representing sky and the presence of the Great Spirit, the lower half painted yellow to symbolise earth or rock.

The beaded strips are typically Teton, executed in lazy stitch seed beadwork of lanes each eight beads wide (approximately 0.5in/ 1.27cm). On white panels, the major motifs seen here (front, top to bottom) are light blue crosses edged with red, with black and white central blocking; black bars crossed by light blue stripes edged red, bearing yellow blocks; yellow crosses edged black, with white and red central blocking; and a repeat of the second motif.

The use of hairlock fringes, either human or horse, suggests the original owner may have been a warrior of note. Triangular neck flaps, characteristic of Oglala and Brulé warrior shirts, may represent the skinned-out heads of the animals used in the construction of the shirts; or, as Taylor (1988) has suggested, may symbolise the knife sheaths worn around the neck by 18th century warriors. (Author's photograph)

By the mid-20th century the generation born within the old culture were passing on. Now poverty, inertia, and the appalling mismanagement of Indian affairs by the government bureaucracy which ran the reservation services and policies (the Bureau of Indian Affairs) found the Indian people at their lowest point. However, the gradual rejuvenation of Indian culture which has occurred since World War II is a powerful mixture of various tribal customs, dress, ethnic symbols and political awareness. Called 'Pan-Indianism' by social anthropologists, it finds

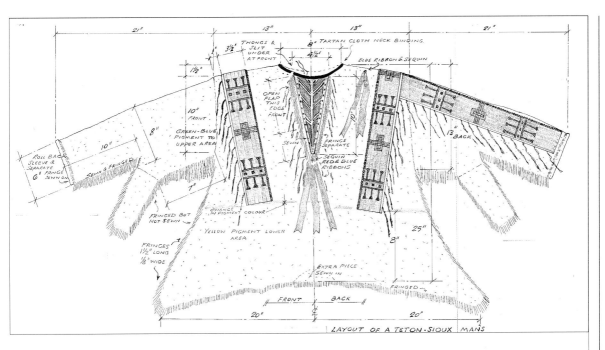

Labels on the drawing: 21″, 13″, 13″, 21″, TARTAN CLOTH NECK BINDING, THONGS & SLIT UNDER AT FRONT, 3½", BLUE RIBBON & SEQUIN, 1½", OPEN FLAP THIS EDGE FRONT, 10″ FRONT, 8″, GREEN-BLUE PIGMENT TO UPPER AREA, SEWN, FRINGE SEPARATE, 13″ BACK, ROLL BACK SLEEVE & SEPARATE 6″ FRINGE SEWN ON, SEWN & FRINGED, 10″, SEQUIN REDR & BLUE RIBBONS, 7″, FRINGED BUT NOT SEWN, CHANGE IN PIGMENT COLOUR, YELLOW PIGMENT LOWER AREA, FRINGES 1½″ LONG ⅛″ WIDE, 25″, 8″, EXTRA PIECE SEWN IN, FRINGED, FRONT BACK, 20″, 20″, LAYOUT OF A TETON·SIOUX MANS

ABOVE **Layout of the Teton Sioux man's buckskin shirt, c1885, now in the Museum of Archaeology and Anthropology at Cambridge University. (Author's drawing)**

its outward expression in the revival of Indian celebrations on all Sioux reservations – the ubiquitous powwow. Male dancers – known as 'Fancy Dancers' or 'Traditional Dancers' – wear baroque regalia using roaches, huge feather bustles, beadwork in matching sets of armbands, cuffs, aprons, and moccasins in various forms, and perform to the songs of specialist singers (see Plate H). Women have revived full-beaded yoke dresses in multicoloured beadwork and younger girls sport the popular 'jingle dress', an adaptation of the Chippewa (Ojibwa) form. The powwow involves parades and formally organised categories of male and female dances which show their Indian dress to advantage.

Men's ceremonial society attire

Members of the Strong Heart and No Flight military societies wore headdresses consisting of buckskin skullcaps covered with ermine skin fringes. At each side split buffalo horns were attached, and beneath them were bunches of owl feathers. At the back was a feathery rudder of black and white eagle feathers. Some of the members carried ring-shaped rawhide rattles, and straight lances decorated with a row of eagle feathers attached to a strip of red trade cloth. The society names refer to the bravery in battle of their members, who did not retreat when attacked.

The old Grass Dance Society adopted from the Omaha Indians probably during the 1860s seems to have incorporated strong elements of older Sioux ceremonialism, with appointed officers and distinctive dancers' dress. Some dancers were entitled to wear a type of back bustle, attached at hip level with a belt

which was sometimes a Hudson's Bay Company yarn sash. The bustle consisted of a rawhide base surmounted by two eagle wing feathers standing upright or outwards. Hanging down were two pieces of heavy red or blue trade cloth with eagle tail feathers attached so that they would flutter gracefully when the dancer moved. On the base, crow, owl or hawk feathers or skins were attached to give the bustle-like effect. Crows, being the first bird to scavenge a battlefield, were thus symbolically associated with warfare, and their use in the construction of these ritual belts has given rise to their alternative name 'crow belts', the crow being one of the guardians of Sioux warriors. The name Grass Dance itself derives from the use of sweetgrass braids worn or tucked in the belt.

From the old Grass Dance dress has descended the modern male powwow dancers' dress with their huge back bustles, but the porcupine and deerhair headroach is a survival from the past. The headroach probably preceded the Grass Dance amongst the Teton and had been reported in use amongst the Santee from the early days of European contact. The fur fillet head-dress was also used by Santee and Yankton men. Sometimes Warbonnet and Buffalo Dances were performed with the old Grass Dance. Both male and female leaders wore eagle feather warbonnets (a ritual probably descended from the older Scalp or Victory Dances), and in the Buffalo Dance men and women wore headdresses of bison scalps with horns. In the Heyoka Dance, usually performed during the Grass Dance, clowns dressed in ragged costume, sometimes with masks, performed strange antics, dancing backwards, carrying crooked bows or bent arrows. These 'clowns' were usually men who had dreamed of the Thunderbird and were holy with the power to heal. During the Sun Dance, male dancers were naked except for a deerskin or cloth kilt and breechcloth and their

(continued overleaf)

sacred ornaments, consisted of a chaplet of sage with horn-like feathers projecting at the sides and scratching sticks attached to the back. Sun Dancers wore their hair loose and unbraided. Other ornaments included wristlets of sage and rabbit fur anklets. Around the neck each carried on a cord an eagle bone whistle upon which he piped while dancing.

Sioux ceremonial shirts and leggings

The basic construction of the Plains Indian ceremonial shirt required two large skins of elk, pronghorn or deer. The lower two-thirds of each skin (the back leg ends) form the main front and back sections, and the upper third (the foreleg ends) formed the arms. These skins were then sewn, laced or held together with buckskin ties. This form, with many variations, was used by all the Teton Sioux branches, as well as the Yankton, Yanktonai, Sisseton and Wahpeton, although examples from the latter three divisions tend to show more tailoring of the skins, even in early specimens. A secondary feature was the addition of neck flaps, perhaps based originally on skinned-out animal heads, or a derivative of the ancient custom amongst the Eastern Sioux of wearing a triangular-shaped knife sheath at the neck.

The outstanding characteristic of Sioux shirts was the use of porcupine-quilled strips, of separate hide, sewn on along the arms and over the shoulder in a vertical plane; this runs contrary to the tradition of horizontal painting on some Subarctic and Woodland attire. Some authorities speculate that this might be traceable to an early European influence on Indians and Métis on the north-eastern margins of the Plains, where the use of European-style epaulettes on the shoulder seams is known in examples of marginal Cree and Métis coats of the late 18th century. Diminutive strips fixed along the shoulder seam of shirts attributed to the Assiniboine, Yanktonai and Santee tend to support this theory.

Ceremonial shirts from the Oglala and Brulé show a predominance of human- and horsehair lock fringes, indicating a strong association with war, rank and status, as also recorded by the use of such shirts by the Chiefs' Societies (Wicasas). Many were painted, the lower half of

the front and back in yellow or red to symbolise earth or rock, and the upper half in blue or blue-green, representing sky. More typical of northern Teton, Yanktonai and Sisseton shirts of the early to mid-19th century were the use of painted warrior figures and equestrian battle scenes. Quilled chest discs, the use of blue pony beads and red flannel cloth neck flaps reflect a mixed style, perhaps shared with the other riverine groups involved in the 19th century Missouri River trade. By about the 1870s the ceremonial shirt had lost its important military status and was replaced gradually by more tailored forms, or by the use of fully beaded vests of Euro-American form.

Early male leggings were also constructed from a complete skin for each legging. The bottom tabs derived from the shape of the skinned-out head of the animal. Later deerskin leggings cut in rectangular shapes and folded to form a tapered tube with flaps – based on the 'cowboy' chaps of the Spanish-Americans – became popular. These were replaced in their turn by similarly constructed leggings of blue or red trade cloth. Along the folded seams were added strips of quillwork (porcupine and bird quills) and hairlock fringes, or strips of beadwork on later leggings. Buckskin shirts and leggings are rarely made today.

Western Sioux women's dress

Teton women were the makers of the magnificent ceremonial male and female attire, work which included tanning deer and elk hides, sewing and decorating – except when painted pictographic warrior figures were used, which seem to have been the preserve of men. There is little evidence that Western Sioux women wore the shoulder strap or single-seam side-fold dresses associated with the Santee and Yankton respectively, at least not for long after their arrival on the High Plains. The oldest known Teton form of skin dress was the full length two-skin form in the original animal shapes, simply folded at the top (the tail end) to give a cape-like effect when the excess flaps were folded down. The classic form of the period before 1850 was similar, but the yoke was a separate piece of skin covering the shoulders and

Sioux women c1920. The women on the left are wearing cloth dresses with belts decorated with German silver; two seated women wear buckskin dresses with beaded capes.

cut to follow the shape of the top or tail edge of the main front and back skins. This so-called 'three-skin' dress was known with variations throughout the Plains and Plateau areas. These dresses give a cape-like shoulderpiece falling over the arms. The side seams were usually sewn and fringed, the forelegs and bottom edge also fringed.

Later, perhaps beginning about 1860 and coinciding with the wide availability of seed beads, the shoulderpiece or yoke became larger, adjoining the skirt skins in a straight line below the bust, and became the fields for exquisite decoration in beadwork. Surviving museum examples have been interpreted as containing symbolical elements from Sioux beliefs. The beadwork in 'lazy stitch' tended to follow the contours of the shoulder yoke in horizontal lanes. As examples of old Sioux dresses with fully quilled yokes are unknown, we have little knowledge about the origins of the beaded designs; but the early 'pony' beaded designs were simply blocks, triangles and diamonds from which complex geometrical seed bead designs later developed. Today Sioux women still make and wear fully beaded yoke dresses, but have added huge amounts of long fringe under the arms, which sway gracefully when dancing.

From around 1880 Sioux women began to wear blue wool trade cloth dresses having large square wings or open sleeves and long triangular insets in the sides of the skirt, which projected below the bottom edge in the manner of the animal leg projections on skin dresses. The shoulders were sometimes sloping to accommodate concentric lanes of dentalium shells. The belts usually worn with cloth dresses had large German silver conches attached, with a tapered pendant. Beaded belts often had a knife case, an awl case, and a strike-a-light pouch and whetstone pouch hanging from them. During the late 19th century Sioux women's leggings of buckskin were tied below the knee, and were often solidly beaded, with a vertically beaded area in front or slightly towards the outside of the leg. Moccasins were of the hard-soled type, usually solidly beaded and occasionally matching the leggings.

Warbonnets

The eagle feather warbonnet has become strongly asso-ciated with the Western Sioux, probably because a number of Teton men joined the 'Wild West' shows of Buffalo Bill, Pawnee Bill and others in the late 19th century and wore them in their circus performances of mock battles. However, by this time they had lost their political and military symbolism and emerged rather as an emblem of 'Indianness', and as such were adopted by many tribes as an ethnic badge.

Eagle and other feathered headdresses were used by many eastern tribes, but they seem to have been constructed by fixing the feathers to a headband to hold them rigidly upright – a form that continued amongst the Blackfoot, Cree and Flathead until reservation days. The bonnet style with feathers sloping backwards, fixed by lacing the feathers to a skullcap, with another control thong passing through each quill in a circle, seems to have developed amongst the Missouri valley tribes and the Crows in the early 19th century. Certainly, by the time the

Paul Strange Horse, Brulé Sioux c.1905. He wears a quilled shirt, a hairpipe-breastplate, and holds a beaded pipebag. His war-bonnet of eagle tail feathers is of the typical Sioux flaring or sloping back style.

artists Catlin and Bodmer were making their records in the 1830s they had already developed into their flaring style.

The Sioux and other central Plains tribes had a complex feather heraldry. Some have suggested that each feather represented a man's scalplock, and certainly each feather did represent some war honour. Most bonnets had between 26 and 36 eagle tail feathers (although sometimes primaries and secondaries). The skullcap used as a basic foundation was originally made of skin, but later cut-down white men's felt hats were used. Each feather was prepared by forming a loop by cutting and turning the thick end of the quill inside itself; in later times an attached rawhide loop was substituted. Near the quill ends were attached eagle 'fluffy' feathers, and red trade cloth wrappings then covered the loop and fluffy bindings. At the tip of the feather horsehair was attached with gypsum or later with sealing wax. Each feather was then laced to the skull cap; a second lacing controlled the feathers to create a flared profile and prevented them blowing forward over the wearer's face. A browband of quillwork or beadwork was usually sewn along the front. Sometimes, from the centre of the back, a stripped quill decorated with fluffy eagle feathers was attached. Sometimes enough feathers were awarded to enable single or double trailers to be added at the back of the bonnet, laced to a red cloth base which was attached to the skull cap, and reaching the ground. However, many such magnificent headdresses were made after the loss of feather symbolism.

Even today warbonnets are still vaguely associated with war, and only chiefs and military veterans are regarded as rightful wearers at today's powwows and Indian celebrations. Ironically, they have decreased in popularity amongst the Sioux, and are rarely seen today at the ceremonials of the people who once made them so popular. However, the Crow and Blackfoot continue to wear them on special occasions.

BIBLIOGRAPHY

Bray, K.M., 'Making the Oglala Hoop: Oglala Sioux Political History, Part I: 1804-1825', *English Westerners' Society, American Indian Studies Series No.2* (1982)

Bray, K.M., 'Making the Oglala Hoop: Oglala Sioux Political History, Part II: 1825-1841, & Part III: 1841-1850', *English Westerners' Society, American Indian Studies Nos. 4 & 5* (1985)

Carley, Kenneth, *The Sioux Uprising of 1862,* The Minnesota Historical Society, St Paul (1976)

Case, Ralph Hoyt, *One Hundred and First Anniversary of the Treaty of Fort Laramie 1851,* National Press Building, Washington, DC (1952)

Ewers, J.C., 'Hairpipes in Plains Indian Adornment, a study in Indian and white ingenuity', *Anthropological Papers No. 50,* Bureau of American Ethnology, Bull.164 (1957)

Hail, Barbara A., *Hau, Kola, The Plains Indian Collection of the Haffenreffer Museum of Anthropology* (1980)

Howard, James H., *The Dakota or Sioux Indians, a Study in Human Ecology published by the Dakota Museum,* University of South Dakota, Vermilion, South Dakota (1966)

Howard, James H., *The Canadian Sioux,* University of Nebraska Press, Lincoln & London (1984)

Meyer, Roy W., *History of the Santee Sioux, United States Indian Policy on Trial,* University of Nebraska Press (1967)

Powers, William K., *Oglala Religion,* University of Nebraska Press (1975)

Smith, J.L., 'A Short History of the Sacred Calf Pipe of the Teton Dakota', *Museum News,* University of South Dakota, Vermillion, South Dakota (July-August 1967)

Tanner, Helen Hornbeck (ed), *Atlas of Great Lakes Indian History,* University of Oklahoma Press (1987)

Taylor, C.F., 'Wakanyan: Symbols of Power and Ritual of the Teton-Sioux', *The Canadian Journal of Native Studies,* Brandon University, Brandon, Manitoba (1988)

Wallis, Wilson D., 'The Canadian Dakota, Vol.41: Pt 1', *Anthropological Papers of the American Museum of Natural History,* New York (1943)

Sioux Sun Dance, early 20th century; male dancers before the centre pole inside the Sun Dance Lodge. (Postcard, author's collection)

THE PLATES

A: COSTUME, c1825-50

A1: Teton Sioux man, c1850

He wears a ceremonial shirt and leggings of antelope, elk or deer skins. The earliest known shirts were of simple 'poncho' style, retaining the original shapes of the animal skins, but sometimes complex forms used more than three hides laced or sewn together. Leggings were simply folded skins with the animals' legs visible at the feet. The shirt and leggings are decorated with strips of porcupine quillwork, the edges of which have fringes of quill-wrapped horse- or human hair 'dangles' – very characteristic of Oglala and Brulé 'shirt-wearers' or chiefs' societies. The neck flap is a truncated triangular shape, also a common trait in ceremonial shirts from the Western Sioux branches. He also wears porcupine-quilled moccasins, and a breechclout of traded stroud cloth. Eagle feather warbonnets were already made in the flaring, back-sloping style when painted by George Catlin in the 1830s. The bonnet brow band and the edges of quillwork strips were sometimes edged with blue 'pony beads'.

Bows were usually of ash, with notched ends for the string of twisted sinew. They were also recurved, and backed with pericardium and sinew, for extra power. Arrows had triple fletchings tied top and bottom with sinew, and small flint heads; metal points shaped from hoop iron were used later. The ash shafts were incised or painted with wavy ownership lines. Short bows were easy to use on horseback and proved deadly weapons – better than percussion firearms; but they were largely discarded for warfare by the 1870s with the arrival of the breech-loading rifle (only a handful of arrowheads have been found on the Custer battlefield).

A2: Teton Sioux woman and child, c1830

Based on a painting by Karl Bodmer c1833, she wears a buffalo robe painted with symbolic designs of 'box-and-border' style. The painting on the robe follows the outline of the untrimmed buffalo hide, and the central design or 'box' is an abstract reference to the internal organs of the animal. Her dress, showing under the robe, may be the rare side-fold type reported from the eastern margins of the Plains. However, the few surviving examples are thought to be Cree, Santee or Yanktonai, and among the Teton Sioux this construction was unknown after the 1830s. Her moccasins are probably the early soft-soled form.

A3: Yanktonai Sioux man, c1830

This shirt is based on a specimen in the Royal Scottish Museum, Edinburgh. It is reputed to have belonged to the noted Yanktonai chief Wanata, and to have been presented to fur traders at Fort Tecumseh (later Fort Pierre); it passed through St Louis at one point, but was reported in Scotland as early as 1837. The shirt and leggings are typical early examples, constructed of deer or antelope hides with only nominal tailoring or fitting. The painted warrior and equestrian figures show the beginnings of European influences in their realism; the porcupine quillwork and maidenhair fern techniques and designs are shared with a number of other museum examples variously attributed to upper Missouri River groups. He holds a traded metal pipe-tomahawk; and also wears a buffalo robe, which were usually painted by men with warrior pictographs and battle scenes. He wears the feathers of various birds of prey in his hair.

Black Eye, Upper Yanktonai Sioux, c1872. Holding pipe and tobacco pouch, he wears a necklace of grizzly bear claws. (Photograph, author's collection)

A4: Santee Sioux girl, c1825

In the 1760s the British fur trader Jonathan Carver illustrated an Eastern Sioux woman's upper garment which appears to be joined over the shoulders by straps. The so-called 'strap dress', sometimes with separate sleeves, seems to have been one of the earliest reported constructions amongst Woodland tribes and those living on the eastern margins of the Plains, e.g. the Plains Cree, Plains Ojibwa and Assiniboine, amongst whom it survived longer. This girl wears a buckskin strap dress based on a museum specimen, collected by Nathan Sturges Jarvis in the 1830s and now in the Brooklyn Museum. She has buckskin leggings decorated with 'pony beads', and porcupine-quilled moccasins.

A5: Yanktonai Sioux earth lodge

The Yankton and Yanktonai are known sometimes to have used earth lodges of a type associated with the Mandan, Arikara and Hidatsa tribes on the Missouri River.

B: CEREMONIAL, c1883

B background: Sun Dance lodge

The lodge was constructed of a circle of upright timbers covered with green branches, reflecting the life forces abundant in spring vegetation. There was an opening on the east side of the lodge facing towards the sun at midday. Rising in the centre of the lodge was the Centre, Sun or Sacred Pole, cut from a living cottonwood tree felled in a sacred manner, and sometimes painted red. Wands of chokecherry wood, sage, sweetgrass, buffalo hair, cloth and other sacred fetishes were hung from the Centre Pole. During the rite, lasting four days (or probably longer in the 19th century) the ceremonies re-created the Sioux world and renewed life for all living things. The piercing, cutting and offerings of the dancers' skin to gain the pity of Wakantanka is thought to be a fairly late development originating amongst the Sioux.

B centre: Sweat lodge

This was a framework of willow saplings covered with robes, blankets or, in recent times, canvas, which symbolically represented the universe. In the centre was built the sacred fire; when this was sprinkled with water the steam rose as 'the breath of life'. Both men and women – although usually separately – underwent purification by sweating in the intense heat; this preceded participation in religious ceremonies. The Sweat Lodge procedure was one of the seven sacred rites of the Sioux, and it survives today among conservative groups.

B foreground: Sun Dance altar and ceremonial pipes

Ceremonial pipes were usually flat or round ash stems covered with plaited and wrapped porcupine quillwork and decorated with horsehair, fur and feathers. The stems were split, grooved and reglued for smoking, or the pith was removed with hot wire. Pipe bowls were usually of redstone 'catlinite', a steatite fashioned at a quarry in Minnesota by Santee and Yankton craftsmen in T, elbow, or effigy forms, and sometimes inlaid with lead or pewter. Buffalo skulls with sweetgrass and sage stuffed in the eyes and mouth formed the altar, with pipes placed on racks in front. Buffalo skulls or their effigies were also attached to the Centre Pole.

B1 & 2: Sun Dancers

Some Sun Dancers (or 'pledgers') were painted and mimicked the movements of dreamed animals: B1 is a black-tailed deer and B2 represents a red deer. Hair ornaments sometimes contained pointed sticks decorated with porcupine quill wrapping and feather pendants. These were used for scratching the body, as dancers were forbidden to touch themselves with their hands. Dancers wore head wreaths, wrist bands and ankle bands made of plaited sage or, in early times, of buffalo fur. It was traditional to let the hair hang loose; and many dancers went barefoot when inside the lodge, wearing moccasins when outside.

Around the neck was suspended an eagle bone whistle, sometimes quilled or beaded; and some dancers wore rawhide cut-outs representing the sunflower (which follows the sun during the earth's orbit). Dancers were bare-chested except for an otter fur cape, but wore a cloth kilt, skirt or clout which reached almost to the ground. Modern Sun Dancers are similarly costumed.

B3: Sun Dance female pledger

Sun Dance pledgers, both male and female, usually made a vow during the previous winter to participate in the rite, in response to a recovery from sickness or release from dreams, out of a desire for revenge or, in recent times, to solicit help with financial or alcohol problems. Abstinence from food and water during the ceremony was obligatory. She wears a trade cloth dress decorated with elk teeth and buffalo hair wrist bands, and holds a sage wreath.

B4: Elk Society dancer

Members of this society had dreamed of bull elks who possessed special powers over the females of their kind; the Elk Dreamers Society therefore had the greatest power for winning women's hearts. When dancing the men wore triangular masks made of young elk or buffalo skin, with cottonwood branches trimmed to represent antlers and sometimes covered with otter fur. They also carried hoops, sometimes with cross cords supporting a mirror in the centre, and covered with elk skin.

C: THE HORSE

Early Spanish explorers such as Ponce de León, De Soto and Coronado have been reported to have left behind strayed horses; but most historians believe that the introduction of horses to native use began through trade with the colonial Spanish in Sonora c1567 and around Santa Fé by 1600. During the 17th century the descendants of these horses spread north by intertribal trade and in wild herds. These probably included a significant strain of the semi-Arab Andalusian horse, and the emerging Indian pony was a typical product of indiscriminate breeding, the result being a small, tough, big-barrelled horse with a blotched hide. The routes north remain a matter of some debate, but the western Sioux probably obtained their first horses between 1720 and 1750, directly from the south – not from the west, the Rocky Mountain route, as did the northern tribes. Before the arrival of the horse the Indians on the margins of the High Plains used dogs as pack animals and to pull the *travois*. The arrival of huge horse herds transformed their lifestyle, allowing them considerable mobility to follow the buffalo and to raid rival tribes. The Plains Indian became the perfect hunting and fighting unit with the merging of horse and warrior, whose manoeuvres on horseback allowed the quick release of arrows or the effective use of lance and club. Though horses remain popular among the Sioux today, the distinctive Indian pony had disappeared by 1940.

Little Wound, Oglala Sioux, wearing a trailer war-bonnet and beaded shirt with hairlock fringes. Photographed by Heyn during the Trans-Mississippi Exposition, Omaha, 1898. (Author's collection)

C1: Mounted Teton Sioux warrior, 1870s

He carries a combined buckskin bow-and-arrow case and a tobacco bag. His horse has a quilled face mask and its tail is decorated with trade cloth (or sometimes with red cloth and eagle feathers – a sign of war). The warrior's shield is also displayed. His shirt has quilled strips, based on a known Brulé specimen.

C2: Teton Sioux woman with cradle and travois, 1870s

The woman sits on a saddle with pommel and cantle, derived from Spanish models. The horse pulls a travois – two poles lashed in a V-shape to support a wooden or lattice platform – carrying 'possible bags', storage containers, parfleche cases and tipi furniture. The artist/explorer George Catlin observed in the 1830s that both horse- and dog-drawn travois were in use during his stay with the Sioux on the Missouri River. The horse has metalwork decorations on its bridle, and beaded saddlebags hang over its flanks. The woman, wearing a quill-decorated robe, holds a porcupine-quilled cradle.

C3: Parfleche bags

These were painted rawhide envelopes used to store meat or clothing.

C4: Sioux tipis

The arrival of the horse allowed the transportation of heavier, and hence bigger, buffalo hide tipis. The basis was a three-pole tripod, with some ten additional poles slotted in. In plan the cover was a near half-circle, and when erected on the frame of lodge-poles it formed a tilted cone, staked down round the edge. Some tipis were decorated with painted warrior pictographic scenes, war records or religious symbols. Two 'ears' (smoke flaps) were held by two external poles, adjusted for wind direction. Inside a secondary wall or liner was used, although it has recently been suggested that this 'dew cloth' only became common in the early reservation period after skin tipis had been replaced by canvas covers. The Sioux lost a great deal of tipi equipment during the Indian Wars, as the US Army forced continual camp moves in their determined campaign to break Sioux resistance.

D: MALE COSTUME, c1860-90

D1: Teton Sioux man, c1890

He wears an immature eagle feather warbonnet, which were used without the military obligations of the 'old days' when appearing in 'Wild West shows' or at Fourth of July celebrations. Over a white man's shirt he wears a 'hairpipe' breastplate of bone tubes obtained from traders, and otter skin set with mirrors. Indians had adopted gauntlets, arm bands, cuffs, collars and ties from the US military, but covered them with beadwork. His blue cloth blanket is edged with yellow ribbon (or selvedge-edged), and a blanket strip of beadwork is sewn across it. Beaded leggings and moccasins complete his outfit. He holds an eagle wing fan, a beaded tobacco pouch/pipe bag, and his ceremonial pipe.

D2: Yanktonai Sioux man, c1875

Skin warrior and society shirts continued to be made and worn during the second half of the 19th century, although they tended to have partly tailored sleeves and bodies.

Western Sioux shirt, c1860 (rear). This shirt was worn by various tribal diplomats in Washington: Red Cloud, American Horse, Touch-the-Clouds (see page 20) and Little Big Man were all photographed wearing it. It is now in the Buffalo Bill Historical Center, Cody, Wyoming. A fine hide shirt with beaded strips and heavy decoration of hairlock fringes, it is painted blue (upper part) and yellow (lower part). The beaded neck flap – basically of red, white, black, dark blue and light blue beadwork with light green and yellow details – is a V-shape divided into two at the bottom, possibly to indicate the wearer's status and office (see Taylor, 1988). The beaded strips at shoulder and arm are basically white edged with dark green, with light blue and dark blue, and blocked lines of red, yellow and light blue. The small quartered blocks on the blue torso are light blue/yellow and red/white. (Author's photograph, 1997)

Buckskin or cloth leggings with outstanding flaps had replaced skin-tight tube leggings. Beaded strips replaced quillwork but painted ornamentation representing individual feats continued to be used. This Yanktonai man has a stroud cloth trade blanket with a wide beaded strip slung over his shoulder, and holds a buckskin gun case with beaded decoration. Note his huge necklace of bear claws, and the dentalium shell hair ornaments characteristic of Yankton and Yanktonai men. The Sioux regarded the bear as a source of great power.

D3: Santee Sioux man, 1860s

The native dress of Santee men reflected their geographical proximity to the Missouri valley, Woodland and Prairie tribes. Moccasins were front-seam or vamped types, and leggings of buckskin; where trade cloth had replaced hide for the latter, they retained the 'front' seams. Our model carries a gunstock-shaped war club, and a large quilled pipe stem with cut-out slats. He has a quilled knife case slung at his throat, a Sioux style reported as early as the mid-18th century. His cloth aprons are decorated with cut-and-fold ribbonwork, a craft virtually unknown among the Western Sioux. He wears Hudson's Bay Company sashes for a belt and a turban; these were copied from earlier Indian-made fibre and wool sashes.

D4: Teton Sioux boy, c1885

He wears a porcupine hair headroach, and his hair is wrapped with otter fur. His vest is quilled in floral designs, adopted by Sioux mixed-bloods from c1875 from trading contacts along the Missouri River. His breechclout and leggings are also of trade cloth. He holds a 'horse memorial' dance stick in honour of a horse killed in battle.

E: FEMALE COSTUME, c1870-90

E1: Teton Sioux woman, 1870
By the 1870s the 'three-skin' buckskin woman's ceremonial dress was often fully beaded over the cape. These 'yokes' (sometimes separate pieces) sometimes bore symbolic female designs – e.g. the U-shaped abstract motif here which refers to the turtle, a female protective symbol. The beadwork was by now being refined into increasingly complex geometrical designs using the imported Italian 'seed beads', which gave the women a huge range of colours in which to practice their art. The Sioux were also capable metalworkers, and our figure shows a belt with 'German silver' conches. Note her dentalium shell earrings and elk tooth necklace. She holds a bone or elk antler hide-scraper with a flint or iron blade, used to scrape the fatty tissue from the inner, or the hair from the outer side of buffalo and deer hides.

E2: Santee Sioux woman, 1860-80
The native dress of the Santee groups resembled that of their neighbours the Winnebago, Sac and – to a lesser extent – Ojibwa. They were in contact with white traders from the 18th century and with Canadian Métis from the early 19th century. Women wore cloth blouses and wrap-around skirts, decorated for ceremonial occasions with either beadwork or ribbonwork. The Santee also absorbed a considerable amount of Cree, Plains Ojibwa and Métis material culture, particularly following the Minnesota war of 1862-63 when many Santee took up residence in Manitoba and Saskatchewan.

E3: Yanktonai Sioux woman, 1880
She wears a trade cloth dress, with projecting tabs at the lower sides which echo the animal legs of earlier skin dresses. The whole upper part is covered with dentalium shells. She also wears a 'tack' belt (leather decorated with brass tacks), from which hang a beaded knife case and a 'strike-a-light' pouch. Vertically strung bone 'hairpipes' reaching down as far as the knee were popular amongst the Yanktonai and also with Teton women. She holds a buffalo calf skin workbag and a painted rawhide container.

E4: Teton Sioux girl, 1890
Based on a photograph of Kate Blue Thunder (Kate Roubideaux), she wears a buckskin dress, leggings and moccasins completely covered with sinew-sewn 'lazy stitch' beadwork in geometric patterns, including US flag motifs; the complex filigree designs were a late 19th century development. Sioux moccasins had hard rawide soles, and forked tongues were common on Teton examples. Note that she carries a doll with a carefully worked costume.

E5: Santee Sioux bark lodge
The Santee Sioux retained their semi-permanent Woodland-style villages comprising bark lodges with pitched roofs and platforms for storing maize. They also used tipis as auxiliary or summer dwellings, however - particularly the Sisseton and Wahpeton branches.

F: WARRIOR SOCIETIES

F1: Omaha Society, c1890
Amongst the Missouri River tribes such as the Omaha, Ponca and Pawnee, warrior societies wore distinctive attire usually consisting of a porcupine and deer hair roach (headdress), a bustle or 'Crow Belt', and a circle and trailer of the feathers of birds of prey – whose scavenging of the field after battle provided the symbolic connection with warfare. From the top of the bustle two feathers projected, representing slain warriors – one a friend, the other an enemy. The belt which secured the bustle behind the waist also held braids of plaited sweetgrass – hence the popular name of the characteristic dancing style, the 'Grass Dance'. During the 1860s these ceremonies were adopted from the Omaha tribe by the Western Sioux, who named it the Omaha Dance or Society. In the late 19th century its function became largely social and it was popular during Fourth of July celebrations. It has formed the basis for the continuing male powwow dancing up to modern times. In early reservation days dancers sometimes used long whistles, the open end carved to represent a bird's head. The Crow Owners Society members wore similar bustles of feathers from birds of prey.

F2: Miwatani or Mandan Society, c1870
An important military society of the Teton Sioux, this is said to have originated long ago with a man who dreamed of an owl, in consequence of which its members used only owl feathers to fletch their arrows. At meetings each member carried a rattle made of the dew claws of deer fastened to a beaded stick, as used in many Sioux dances. Warrior society sashes were sometimes pinned to the ground in battle so that there would be no retreat. Quirts notched and carved in a zig-zag pattern to represent lightning bolts were used by officers of several military societies.

F3: Strong Heart Society, c1880
The Strong (or Brave) Heart Society was probably founded by Sitting Bull (our model here), Gall and Crow King. They wore headdresses consisting of buckskin skullcaps covered with fringes of ermine skin, split curved buffalo horns and owl feathers. Some members carried ring-shaped rawhide rattles, and lances decorated with a row of eagle feathers attached to a strip of red trade cloth extending the whole length of the shaft. In their dances they adopted a bobbing, up-and-down movement. Strong Heart Society shields were usually painted with an eagle design and trimmed with eagle feathers.

F4: Fox or Kit Fox Society, c1880
This society was so named because its members were supposed to be wily and active on the warpath. They wore kit-fox skin around the neck and wrist. When dancing they painted their bodies yellow, and held a bow-lance. In battle the bow-lance was driven into the ground and warriors fought under its perceived powers of protection.

G: THE RESERVATIONS

G1: Sioux male Ghost Dancer, c1890
The religious movement popularly known as the Ghost Dance originated in California; it was revived in Nevada, where Sioux emissaries learned the rite from the Paiute tribe, and it gained many adherents amongst the Teton in the Dakotas. As it began to take on a more belligerent stance in the face of

mounting white opposition, specially painted clothes were claimed to give protection against the white man's bullets. The Sioux usually painted their foreheads, cheeks and chins with red ochre. This man's muslin shirt is painted with religious motifs and trimmed with hair fringes; he wears blue stroud cloth leggings with beaded strips, and fully-beaded moccasins. He holds a rawhide drum and its beater.

G2: Sioux female Ghost Dancer, c1890
Sioux Ghost Dance clothes were usually made from muslin, although a few dresses were made from cotton, or even from flour sacks. The religious symbols painted on dresses and shirts had become intermixed with the white man's signs, but eagles, butterflies, dragonflies, four-pointed stars and moons linked the dancers to the natural world. Visions experienced during the ceremony would help the reunion of the dancers with their dead friends and relatives.

G3: Sioux boy, c1890
With Euro-American garments he wears a beaded vest, with pictographic figures of warriors holding US flags, and fully-beaded trousers, with quilled moccasins. After he is taken away from his family to attend public school he will only be allowed to wear white man's clothes.

G4: Sioux baby girl, c1890
A number of Cheyenne families settled with the Sioux at Pine Ridge Reservation; and this lattice-type cradle is more usually associated with the Cheyenne. It is fixed to a wooden frame, with characteristic painted boards decorated with brass tacks; the whole cradle is solidly beaded. On the hood hangs a beaded umbilical cord holder in the shape of a turtle.

G5: Teton Sioux man and woman, c1907
This couple demonstrate the extent to which Sioux women had developed geometrical beadwork patterns. The man has a solidly-beaded vest and trousers, the former based on a specimen which belonged to Andrew Knife, an Oglala from Pine Ridge Reservation, which is now in the Blackmore Collection at the Hastings Museum in England. The woman wears a fully-beaded yoke on her dress, and beaded leggings. Her horse has a beaded saddle blanket and headstall. (Fully-beaded examples of even such items as doctors' bags and violin cases are known.)

H: CONTEMPORARY POWWOW COSTUME
H1: Contemporary male dancer, c1988
During the 1970s a new style of men's dance dress developed amongst the Western Sioux, who by this time preferred their own name for themselves in the Western dialect – 'Lakota'. It has become known as 'contemporary traditional' dress, because it uses elements of early dance dress – e.g. porcupine and deer hair headdress, beaded arm bands and cuffs, 'hairpipe' breastplates, eagle feather bustle, angora anklets, and solidly-beaded cape and moccasins. This figure is based upon a dancer seen by the artist at Eagle Butte, Cheyenne River Reservation, in 1988. He is believed to have been a veteran of the Vietnam War.

H2: Flag bearer, c1980
A Vietnam veteran whose status fitted him to carry the US flag during the Grand Entry at a modern 'Lakota' Powwow.

He wears combat fatigues (camouflage BDUs); and a beret with a red-dyed eagle feather, indicating that he was wounded in battle.

H3: Contemporary male dancer, c1995
This dancer wears a wolfskin on his head decorated with red-tailed hawk feathers and quilled hoops. He has a fully-beaded vest, arm and knee bands, cuffs, brass sleigh bells, angora anklets and beaded moccasins. This style of dance dress has become very popular amongst men of many tribes from Canada to Oklahoma, and represents a distinctively 'Lakota' contribution to Pan-Indianism.

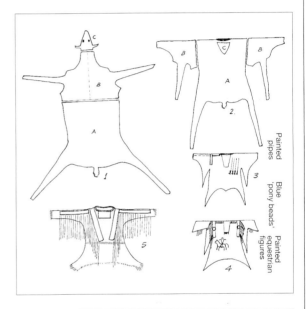

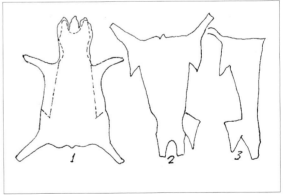

TOP **Western Sioux ceremonial shirts of 'poncho' type.**
(1) Basic construction from two skins
(2) Arrangement of skins to form the shirt – 2 x A, 2 x B
(3) Early shape with small shoulder strips
(4) Early shape with quilled strips, disc and hair fringe
(5) Mid-/late 19th C, back view – part tailored, with beaded strips and buckskin fringe
ABOVE **Early skin leggings: (1) Basic skin and cut**
(2) With added gusset (3) Folded legging

INDEX